MODERN GERMAN LITERATURE
The Major Figures in Context

For the students in my seminar

1964 – 1965

MODERN GERMAN LITERATURE

The Major Figures in Context

by Henry Hatfield

New York
St Martin's Press
1967

© Henry Hatfield 1966
First published 1966
First published in
the United States of America in 1967

Library of Congress Catalog Card Number : 67-11839

Printed in Great Britain by
William Clowes and Sons, Limited, London and Beccles

Contents

5000

Preface

In German literature, the twentieth century stands out as a vital and productive period. In a sense, one may say that the century started some ten years ahead of schedule, for fresh impulses began to make themselves felt in Berlin and Vienna around 1890. From that time until 1933, literary life was particularly vigorous. Even during the Hitler period, exiled writers produced many admirable works and a few great ones; and since about 1947 there has been evidence of a genuine revival in Germany itself.

Since any historical account of literature involves criticism, I have often ventured to make value judgments in this book, rather than writing a neutral account or trying to explain developments in terms of cause and effect. As Wellek and Warren have put it, '. . . causal study can never dispose of problems of description, analysis, and evaluation of . . . a work of literary art.' Agreeing with Emil Staiger that criticism is impossible if the critic suppresses his own reactions, I have tried all the more to separate opinions very clearly from facts. The only hope of approximating objectivity lies in stating one's own point of view openly, but to be as fair and accurate as one can.

Since this is a selective account, I have chosen a relatively small number of writers for discussion. (For fuller treatments of the period, one can turn to *Dichtung und Dichter der Zeit* by Albert Soergel and Curt Hohoff or Jethro Bithell's *Modern German Literature*.) Even in a book of this length, it would have been possible to include twice as many authors as I have here, but at the cost of undue curtness, perhaps of sketchiness. Doubtless several of my exclusions and inclusions will surprise or annoy various readers: what seems selective to one student may strike another as arbitrary.

In organizing a bewilderingly rich and varied body of literature, I have tried to use the approaches suitable to its several parts. Accordingly, three groups of writers who were keenly aware that they were members of a literary school—the naturalists, expressionists, and, to a lesser extent, the neo-romanticists—are treated in chapters of their own. In most other instances, literary works are arranged by genre. As the situation of writers during the 'nightmare years' 1933–45 was unique, I have treated it in a brief 'interchapter' stressing political and social conditions. Of course, my method could be called eclectic; but one has to use more than one tool when faced with a complicated job.

To avoid splitting into small fragments my treatment of writers who played a part in more than a single period or 'ism,' I have disregarded chronological chapter limits in a few cases. Thus it seemed convenient to discuss the late works of Heinrich and Thomas Mann, Gerhart Hauptmann, and Hermann Hesse together with their publications of the Weimar period. Similarly, since Stefan George published only one volume of verse after 1918, I considered it with his earlier ones. Thus while, in a few cases, a major author has been discussed in two different chapters, fragmentation has been minimized.

It is often surprisingly difficult to give the precise date for the publication of a given work. In many instances, one highly respected authority will differ from another. Rather than cluttering up these pages with a host of dates, I have tried to furnish enough to make the time sequence clear. To complement these, the 'Index' (pp. 159 ff.) gives the dates of all the works discussed in the text. Unless otherwise noted, the date supplied is that of first publication.

Naturally I am indebted to the literary histories of Jethro Bithell, Victor Lange, Claude David, and Soergel-Hohoff—especially to the latter two. As the Notes show, I also owe much to many more specialized works. It is a pleasure to acknowledge a particular debt to Heinz Politzer's *Kafka*, Theodore Ziolkowski's *Hesse*, and Martin Esslin's *Brecht*.

I owe thanks to the staffs of the Harvard College Library and the Baker Library of Dartmouth College for courteous and efficient assistance. For information and comment, I am grateful to Ritta-Jo Horsley, who gave every chapter a sympathetic but close reading, and to Walter Grossmann, Wolfgang Paulsen, Winthrop Root, Robert Spaethling, and Jack Stein—all of whom read and commented on one or more chapters of this book—as well as to Bernhard Blume, Crane Brinton, Ruth and Peter Gay, Harry Levin, and Eckehard Simon. Ingeborg Harris helped me in many ways, above all by checking hundreds of dates, and Sigrid Johnson typed the last version of the MS with great accuracy. Barbara Hatfield subjected the style of my first draft to an examination valuable in its severity. Above all I must thank my wife for typing most of the first draft and especially for criticism and encouragement.

Harvard University
January, 1966

Henry Hatfield

Acknowledgement

The author and publishers wish to thank Martin Secker and Warburg, Ltd., and Franz J. Horch, Inc., for their kind permission to include two extracts from *Man without Qualities* by Robert Musil.

1   *Art as Nature: Naturalism*

"Die Kunst hat die Tendenz, wieder die Natur zu sein . . . ."
                                                    —*Arno Holz*

Around 1880 German literature* was at the lowest point it had reached in over a century. As Nietzsche insisted, the victorious war with France seemed to have ruined German culture at the same time that it established the power and prosperity of the new empire. While many writers were active, most of them lacked taste and a sense of form; even the few formalists, correct talents like Emanuel Geibel or Paul Heyse, now seem mere imitators, epigones, to use a term significantly current ever since Goethe had died, some fifty years before. For almost a score of years around mid-century, not a single highly gifted creative writer was born in Germany.[1]

Even more depressingly, the very genres seemed tired: above all, the literary forms which had been the great glory of the Age of Goethe: the lyric, the poetic drama, the novel of education (*Bildungsroman*). Yet by 1900 the situation was radically different; writers of genius, like Thomas Mann, Rilke, and Hofmannsthal, had emerged—some would include Stefan George, Gerhart Hauptmann, and perhaps Hermann Hesse as well in the first rank— and a whole galaxy of lesser but indubitably lucent stars—men like Wedekind, Schnitzler, Heinrich Mann, and so on. Moreover, there were hundreds if not thousands of literary men of some modest distinction; at the very least, they formed the core of an intelligent reading public. An authentic if perhaps minor renascence was under way. By 1914, when the long-threatening catastrophe finally struck, German literature was as stimulating as that produced by any contemporary culture. A large, gifted (and often noisy) expressionist school had sprung up in literature as in the fine arts. Particularly in

* In this book, German literature denotes all literature written in the German language, regardless of political or geographical factors. In cases where a specifically Swiss or Austrian strain is important, it will be mentioned.

the drama and the lyric, its members vied with the older writers. Something like a cultural explosion was under way.

To turn back, briefly, to the literary situation around 1880. In the lyric, the major romantic tradition of writing more or less in the manner and spirit of the folk song was wearing thin indeed. It is not too fanciful to regard this type of poetry, after Heine, as a living corpse: when he had extracted its last possibilities he dispatched the simple, or pseudo-simple *gemütlich* song with parody. Too naïve to comprehend his own demise, the blue-eyed simpleton had to be killed again in the Nineties, mainly by George. The 'other' strain of the German lyric, deriving from one aspect of Goethe's poetry and such figures as Rückert and Platen, elaborate in form and often exotic in both form and theme, was cultivated to great applause by the Munich circle; Geibel and Heyse were its leading virtuosos. Incredibly, or rather all too credibly, Heyse was awarded a Nobel Prize as late as 1910; a distinction granted to none of the great masters of German poetry.[2] In Switzerland, the lyrics of Conrad Ferdinand Meyer form an admirable exception to the general triteness. At their best they are delicate and precise, using imagery with restraint but much effect. It has been ably argued that Meyer is the great German forerunner of European symbolism.[3] Such a poem as 'Zwei Segel' does point in this direction, but one doubts that Meyer's none too vigorous strivings had the impact which the poetry of the great French symbolists from Baudelaire on was to have. (His novellas are praised by nearly all the literary historians; too highly, in most cases.) The North German nobleman, Detlev von Liliencron, is generally hailed as a shining exception and an important precursor of the impressionistic lyric, and he does indeed evoke bright flashes of colour. In his minority opinion that Liliencron has been much over-praised, however, Claude David seems eminently sound.[4] (That this minor figure was a nobleman and a Prussian officer whose works give a glamorous impression of warfare hardly discredited him in the eyes of the nationalistic professors who largely determined the official standing of German writers—at least from 1870 to 1945.)

In the drama, affairs were even more dismal; not even respectable second-raters like Hebbel or Grillparzer survived. A descendant of the Hohenzollerns, Ernst von Wildenbruch, wrote high-flown historical tragedies which tried to continue Schiller's tradition. One doubts that even a Prussian monarchist would read him today. Still lesser figures wrote light plays *à la* Sardou or Augier; they have a place in the history of the entertainment industry, not that of literature. Small wonder that Wagner's operas, faced with such competition, seemed to be what he fondly thought them—great dramas in their own right.

Relatively, the novella was the most successful of German nineteenth-century genres. And although the novel certainly did not flower, it did not go to seed as badly as the lyric or drama. To be sure, one of the very few contemporary masters of German prose, Gottfried Keller, had finished the revision of his only important novel, *Der grüne Heinrich*, by 1880. With it, the distinguished line of the *Bildungsroman* came to a temporary close; though of course many novels of the type were attempted, only Thomas Mann and Hesse were able to revive it. Spielhagen's once highly praised social novels are no longer esteemed, though his theoretical writings about the novel are still interesting. While there were provincial writers of some note, like the Austrian Rosegger, hardly anyone reads them today except perhaps pupils in the schools and *Gymnasia*. Much more rewarding though extremely uneven in quality, Wilhelm Raabe's novels also appear parochial when compared to English, Russian, or French fiction of the nineteenth century.

One admirably sophisticated, sensitive novelist was writing in the Eighties—Theodor Fontane. Perhaps it was impossible to be a great novelist in the nineteenth century without the quality which Thomas Mann called 'the backbone of all literature'—realism.[5] A master realist, Fontane describes a credible society—usually that of Berlin or of the Prussian landed aristocracy—with both sympathy and irony, avoiding the whimsical fancies of a Jean Paul, the tendentiousness of a Spielhagen, and the didacticism of Keller. In the main current of the European novel—not, emphatically, of the German[6]—Fontane focuses on a few scenes and normally on a few characters; he is *not* concerned with tracing a hero's development for hundreds and hundreds of pages—still less with describing and commenting on the young man's Weltanschauung. If Berlin and the surrounding country were as attractive or 'romantic' to many people as are Paris, London, or even New York, Fontane might well have worldwide renown.

One sharp limitation his books do have: he generally shies away from recording scenes of intense passion (or of action) preferring a 'veiling' technique. The influence of his style on Thomas Mann, perhaps through the Baltic writer Eduard von Keyserling, was great.

Despite Fontane and a very few others, then, the Germans had lagged far behind in literature during a time of unexampled prosperity and power. And two of the most gifted writers of the mid-century, Friedrich Nietzsche and Jacob Burckhardt, were not primarily interested in *belles lettres*: both the philosopher and the historian operated on the frontiers of literature. Guides there already were to lead the lost tribe out of the wasteland, but these were men of the North, the West, the Slavic East: Ibsen, Strindberg, Zola, Tolstoy, Dostoevsky. Native voices were also to prove helpful, but not the spokesmen of Bismarckian self-assertion or Philistine self-congratulation. In the Eighties, though, the alienated voices of relative outsiders like Nietzsche and Burckhardt were hardly heard.

Before dealing with the new development which began in the Eighties and became productive a few years later, a few points should be made about the social and political state of Germany and Austria. While the old dream of German unity had been partially fulfilled, it had been realized by means disturbing to many of the more sensitive and conscientious citizens of the new state. By no means all speakers of German were included, though many Poles and Alsatians found themselves reluctant subjects of the Hohenzollerns. Of course the men of 1848 regretted that union came not from the liberal Frankfurt Parliament but from Bismarck's frank, ruthless (and masterly) use of force. Probably 'the power and the glory' of the new state tended to make many repress their moral doubts.

Doubtless the most startling change to take place in Germany in the nineteenth century was the transformation of a largely agricultural region into an enormously powerful, highly organized industrial society. The heavy reparations—5 billion francs—extracted from the French in 1871 proved a powerful if inflationary stimulus. As late as 1850,[7] 'the Germanies' were industrially a second-rate power; with their forests, castles, their old towns clustering around Gothic cathedrals or Baroque churches, many of the German states still seemed romantic, often quaint, almost idyllic. By the end of the century the very landscape had radically changed:

Great cities like Crefeld, Düsseldorf, Elberfeld, Barmen, Essen and Dortmund lie so close together that an automobile will cover the entire circle of them in a day's easy ride, and they are linked together by a chain of busy municipalities which bid fair themselves soon to become important cities. The growth of this region has been almost appalling. The day is blackened by smoke pouring from a hundred stacks, the night is agleam with the angry light of thousands of coke ovens and blast furnaces, the earth trembles under the whizzing of cars laden with coal and iron. New factories have constantly sprung up, equipped with the latest technical contrivances, and whole new streets of workingmen's dwellings lead out from every suburb far into the open country. In the early morning miles of becapped workingmen fill the walkways or bicycle through the streets, in the evening the earth fairly quakes under the tread of the army of labour taking its way homeward.[8]

With help from the protectionist policies of the new Reich, the German entrepreneurs, proverbially energetic, able, and ruthless, built up vast cartels controlled by a few men and competed more and more successfully with the western economies. German goods were everywhere: yet the nation's rulers came to believe that its power in Europe was insufficient; that prestige required colonies, a great navy, a 'place in the sun.'

In an attempt to blunt the appeal of socialism, Bismarck introduced an effective system to protect the workers against the worst effects of unemployment, illness, and old age. While these measures functioned well enough, the 'lower class' maintained a sceptical attitude towards the Prusso-German establishment. Marxism exerted an increasing appeal, influencing the social and political attitudes of many writers and artists of the Eighties. Unfortunately, the Marxist tone of the Social Democratic party badly frightened the remaining German liberals—who had already lost many of their best men to America in the massive emigration of 1848 and following years. However reluctantly, they tended to make common cause with the Ruhr industrialists and even the Junkers, thinking them the lesser evil.

Naturalism, important in France by the 1860's, reached Germany very late, in the Eighties; soon afterward, it was pushed aside by yet another European movement.[9] Not only in France and England but in Russia and Scandinavia a realistic literature had developed, harsher, sterner, and more virile than the vaguely named 'poetic realism' which obtained in most German nineteenth-century fiction between about 1840 and 1880. Balzac, Flaubert, Zola, even Maupassant and the Goncourts; Dickens; Tolstoy and Dostoevsky; Ibsen and Strindberg were more challenging, more *dans le vrai* than writers like Storm, Otto Ludwig, or even the good, grey Keller. Soon the young—or 'youngest' Germans, as they were often called,[10] came to recognise that their literature had lagged behind.

Of course, there were German forerunners of the new development too: the Enlightenment, realistic dramatists of the Storm and Stress, especially Lenz and the young Schiller, the 'Young Germans' of the 1830's and 1840's, Fontane, the Austrian Ludwig Anzengruber, and above all Georg Büchner, whose drastic, incredibly 'modern' plays were published, mainly for the first time, in 1879. He had been dead over forty years, but his works struck the new generation, including Gerhart Hauptmann, with stunning force. This generation rejected only mid-century 'poetic realism,' not the German tradition as a whole.

Largely because of the prestige of natural science, this more 'tough-minded' realism came to be known as naturalism. ('Nature,' after all, had been a shibboleth since the seventeenth century, for men as diverse as Descartes, Goethe, and Wordsworth.) The greatest theorist and the most famous practitioner of naturalism, Emile Zola, defined the work of art as 'a corner of nature seen through a temperament.' Although this definition allows for the subjectivity of the artist, he defined the 'experimental novel'—his literary goal—as the apex of the sciences, combining vigorous objectivity with 'personal expression.' At first, Zola was generally considered immoral by the more conservative German critics, but his practice, especially in his long series of novels *Les Rougon-Macquart* and his theory as expressed in *Le roman expérimental* (1880), were ably expounded and defended by Michael Georg Conrad, the brothers Julius and Heinrich Hart and others. Soon Zola became a canonical figure for the writers of the new school.

The poet and critic Arno Holz was the most extreme of the German naturalists. In his theoretical works he cites and draws upon the positivism of Comte, Taine's triad of inheritance, milieu, and race,[11] and the writings of Buckle, John Stuart Mill, and Herbert Spencer. German theorists like Wilhelm Boelsche and Conrad Alberti generally upheld the scientific positivism of these 'Westerners,' but Georg Brandes, in a brilliant essay on Zola of 1888, emphasized the subjective aspect of his work, and Hermann Bahr and others joined in the assault on naturalistic theory. Precisely this 'anti-scientism' provoked Arno Holz to a very radical statement of the naturalist position. In the interests of science, as he thought, he eliminated the subjective element; 'and that was his undoing.' Almost fanatic in his conviction, he stated that 'art equals nature minus "x"'—'x' representing the artist's subjectivity and the limitation of his medium. Thus the greatest painter would be inferior to any competent photographer. Holz, revising Zola's dogma in the interests of what he called 'consistent naturalism,' was led by the dialectics of the situation to destroy naturalism itself.[12]

Various other paradoxes of naturalism deserve mention. Devoted in principle to the objective neutrality of the laboratory, it was in action and feeling—to its honour—sworn to the cause of the poor and oppressed. Since they were deeply concerned with suffering and squalor, the naturalists were accused of morbid pessimism; actually, as W. H. Root well shows, they harboured an optimistic, one might almost say 'American' belief that rational action can assure to all men the right to 'life, liberty, and the pursuit of happiness.'[13] Less appealing is another naturalistic contradiction: in theory internationally oriented, some of the naturalists took a nationalist stance.

Aside from a very few narratives, the naturalists were really effective only in the drama. Again, as for young Schiller, the theatre became a pulpit, a 'moral institution.' With the opening of the 'Freie Bühne'—modelled on Antoine's 'théâtre libre'—in Berlin, in 1889, the naturalists scored a decisive victory. To evade the censorship, the supporters of the new theatre, which had no building of its own, had to organize themselves as a private club, and it proved feasible to put on only some ten performances a year; but the effect was electric. Opening with Ibsen's *Ghosts*, the 'Freie Bühne' followed it with Hauptmann's *Vor Sonnenaufgang*, which produced a gratifyingly tumultuous reaction. Among other works represented in that first exciting year were Tolstoy's *Power of Darkness* and plays by Strindberg, Björnson, and the Goncourt brothers. Brilliantly directed by Otto Brahm, a man as difficult as he was gifted, the new group had both a *succès de scandale* and genuine success. (Its journal *Freie Bühne für modernes Leben*, eventually rechristened *Die neue Rundschau*, remains the most prestigious German literary magazine.) *Die Moderne*, as the supporters of the movement liked to call it, had arrived. Again Berlin was a centre of genuinely European culture— more so than at any time since the days of Lessing, Moses Mendelssohn, Frederick II, and Voltaire.

Not that the German works put on at the 'Freie Bühne' were particularly memorable. Aside from a few plays by Gerhart Hauptmann and a few others by Arthur Schnitzler, it is doubtful that any naturalistic dramas in German could hold an audience today. But the new seriousness was decisive, and the theme was the thing. Like Brecht, such naturalistic playwrights as Carl Hauptmann, Max Halbe, and Holz (in collaboration with Johannes Schlaf) examined all the more striking social problems of the day.[14] Alcoholism, heredity, the schools (adolescents driven to despair by vicious schoolmasters abound in the novel as well as on stage), the peasantry, orthodoxy vs. free thought, officers vs. civilians, sexual enlightenment, the 'new woman,' and above all the clashes between the generations and between rich and poor become, or again become, matters for theatrical examination. All this is anti-'culinary' enough to satisfy the most rigorous Brechtian, but most of these dramas have two fatal weaknesses: they tend to show dull people, and to be sentimental. (Accordingly they have been linked with the bourgeois drama and the subliterary novel.)[15]

It may be helpful to discuss one of the better of these dramas, *Die Familie Selicke* by Holz and Schlaf (1890), as a fair representative of the genre. Typically elaborate stage directions describe the Berlin flat of a lower-class family; father Selicke (a bitter play on *selig*, 'blissful'?) drinks heavily but means well. His wife is sickly and querulous; of the four children, Linchen, an eight-year old girl, dies just after her father has come home drunk. To increase the poignancy, all this takes place at Christmas. A second daughter, Toni, becomes engaged to their lodger Wendt, who has just been appointed to his first pastorate. (The naturalists often took over from

Ibsen the 'saviour-from-afar' character, in their dramas; but he generally does not save the situation.) After Linchen's death, Toni feels that she must renounce marriage (and thus all hope of escape from misery); Wendt leaves, and although he promises to return, we are not sure of the strength of his determination. At best, there will be a long period of gloomy waiting. Nothing much has happened, except for the death of poor Linchen, when the drama closes not with the bang of the 'well made play' but with the naturalistic whimper.

At times, *Die Familie Selicke* has a certain power. Heaven knows that such families exist, but one feels that they should be drawn with sharper, cleaner lines such as Strindberg and even the expressionist Georg Kaiser employed to show comparable drabness. Typically, we find here an absence of both heroes and villains, the insistence on the importance of milieu (though character flaws are even more decisive), the use of dialect, the depiction of an average bit of life with no particular beginning, middle, nor end. As 'consistent naturalists,' Holz and Schlaf try to report on every second (the well-known *Sekundenstil*) as well as on every detail of the milieu. Unexpectedly, this results in the resurgence of the unities of space and time—it would not be feasible to shift things or people around. The play leaves one not with the conviction that science and rational action could change the lives of the Selickes, but that they are caught in a trap from which there is no escape.

In the fiction of the naturalistic school, performance also failed to keep up with theory. Again, the real merit of these writers is moral and social, not aesthetic: they insist that truth must be told, that the proletarians and the rural poor deserve our interest at least as much as do the more fortunate classes. Their literary accomplishment is a vicarious one: by handing on the ideal of authentic realism to younger, more gifted writers, they helped indirectly to produce works of a quality which they could not attain themselves.

Perhaps the most representative naturalistic novelist is Max Kretzer. Himself a proletarian, he devoted his best novels to the proletariat of Berlin. *Die Betrogenen* (1882) deals with prostitution; *Meister Timpe* (1888; described by the author as a social novel) treats the decline and ruin of a once reasonably prosperous family unable to deal with changed economic and social forces. Like Zola, whom

2

incidentally he denied having read, he made use of striking, at times flamboyant symbolism.

Of course, symbolism and naturalism are not mutually exclusive. One of the few still interesting naturalist stories of the Eighties is Gerhart Hauptmann's 'Bahnwärter Thiel' (1887). Here rigid physical determination is central: Thiel, a railway gatekeeper, who remarried soon after the death of his much-loved first wife, is morally destroyed by his bad conscience and above all by his brutally earthy second wife, who is obviously far more highly sexed than he; his child by the first marriage is killed through her negligence. Yet a sensitive reading shows that Hauptmann's genuinely poetic use of symbols is equally essential to the story: Marianne Ordon has shown that especially the animals, squirrel and deer, lead us to an awareness of the 'unconscious contents' of the story.[16]

A more radical example of naturalistic fiction is the story 'Papa Hamlet' by the indefatigable Holz and Schlaf. Set in Norway, the narrative is ascribed to a 'Bjarne P. Holmsen'—telling evidence of Scandinavian literary prestige—but its characters are clearly German. Again, the action deals with drunkenness and the death of a child; this time by infanticide. Papa Hamlet, a drunken, unemployed actor, who eventually meets his end in a gutter, quotes *Hamlet* in heavily ironic counterpoint to the sordid happenings. Possibly the phonographic reproduction of the various ways of speaking gives this sketch some literary value.

Even the pseudo-naturalist Sudermann wrote in *Frau Sorge* (1887) and *Der Katzensteg* (1889) two very readable novels whose 'realism' was doubtless less diluted by sentimentality, thanks to the influence of *Die Moderne*. His semi-naturalistic dramas *Die Ehre* and *Heimat* were once greatly admired. Better works were to come, thus in the admirably honest narratives of Clara Viebig, like *Kinder der Eifel* (1897). In general, though, the best naturalist German prose of the nineteenth century was written by Arthur Schnitzler,* a man with a genuinely scientific training and attitude who did not feel constrained to talk continually about science. Schnitzler is to Holz as a rapier to a cudgel. Since Schnitzler was not a doctrinaire naturalist, and since, a Viennese *par excellence*, he was more sophisticated and

* See below, pp. 23–26.

far less dogmatic than the writers of the Berlin school of the late Eighties, his work will be discussed with that of his major Viennese contemporaries.

The one great (partially) naturalistic novel in the German language is Thomas Mann's *Buddenbrooks*, a book which far transcends naturalism but shows that the author—at twenty-five—could easily surpass the Holzes and Kretzers (and perhaps even Zola) at their own game. One need instance only the few pages devoted to Hanno's death, to the excruciating visits of Hanno and his father to the dentist, or—on a more cheerful note—the accounts of the Buddenbrooks' menus.

If Emil Staiger is right in holding that the lyric is the expression of pure subjectivity (first person singular, here, now) then the very notion of naturalistic lyric is self-contradictory. Generally the verses of these writers tend to be conventional in form, however 'modern' in content. There is of course a social lyric of the time, devoted to the miseries of the poor. This is laudable but does not necessarily bear on naturalism, unless one would insist that Shelley and Werfel were naturalists too. There is far more naturalism in Brecht's 'A Plum Tree' or even in some of Schiller's distichs than in these efforts; and it was in the lyric that the aesthetic, in a sense anti-realistic spirit, was soon to gain its greatest triumphs, as in the poems of Rilke, George, Hofmannsthal, and Trakl. The early anthology *Moderne Dichtercharaktere* (1885), once highly regarded, is full of mediocre stuff. Later the omnipresent Arno Holz deserted the naturalistic lyric for a pedantically formalistic verse in which every line was centred on the middle of the page, on its axis, as he put it.[17]

By far the most gifted member of the group was Gerhart Hauptmann. After he had published *Vor Sonnenaufgang* (1889) Fontane hailed him, at twenty-seven, as the 'fulfillment of Ibsen.' To the general public he appeared as *the* angry young naturalist, but only four years later he included a strongly neo-romantic note in his social tragedy *Hanneles Himmelfahrt*. His symbolic drama *Die versunkene Glocke* (1896) is the product of a highly self-conscious romanticism—and one of his worst plays, though highly regarded at the time. From that time on Hauptmann more or less alternated, for years, between mainly naturalistic and predominantly neo-romantic, symbolic works.

Such oscillation is typical, and helps one to understand why Hauptmann's position in literary history is less clearly defined than those of most of the other major writers of his generation. Greatly gifted, he is equally uneven. He published over sixty volumes containing novels, novellas, epic poems, lyrics, autobiography, and accounts of his travels as well as dramas of various types. Extraordinarily Protean, he ranged from almost 'consistent' naturalism to hyperromanticism, from the strong sympathy with Christianity expressed in *Der Narr in Christo Emanuel Quint* to the completely pagan sexuality of *Der Ketzer von Soana*. His political record is equally inconsistent. Hauptmann's greatest qualities are his empathetic grasp of character and his unforced compassionateness: 'Judge not!' is a note he sounds again and again. When he strikes an intellectual pose he is at his worst. Mynheer Peeperkorn in Mann's *Der Zauberberg* is by no means an unfair caricature. Hauptmann liked to use philosophical terms without really grasping them. 'The minute he sets up as a thinker, he becomes a child,' Goethe said of Byron; and Byron's mind was far keener than Hauptmann's.

On balance he appears as a vastly talented writer who insufficiently channelled and directed his energies, and who thus failed, aside from a few brilliant exceptions, to realize the promise of his early years. Yet not only was his contribution to naturalism of the greatest importance; there is a consensus that the best of his early dramas, like *Die Weber* and *Der Biberpelz*, are as fine as he ever achieved. They are his finest, I suspect—and stand in the first rank of plays in the German language.

To be sure, *Vor Sonnenaufgang* is immature and at times clumsy; someone has called it Ibsene.[18] The weight of naturalistic ideology and moralizing has sunk it almost completely: there are for instance the infant (alcoholic by the age of three) and the priggish if sincere idealist who deserts his fiancée, apparently with the author's approval, because of her faulty heredity. Even here, though, some of the characters are admirably drawn, and Hauptmann's reproduction of various 'language levels' is masterful.

Only two years later Hauptmann finished *Einsame Menschen*, a play of real power; while he is still indebted to Ibsen, to *Rosmersholm* especially, his own individuality appears in the characteristic sympathy for human suffering and the typically weak hero. (Compared to Hauptmann's neurasthenics and frustrated intellectuals, even the defeated personages in Ibsen seem almost heroic.)

Although his basic situation is that of the all too eternal triangle, Hauptmann's drama conveys a sense of freshness and authenticity. As Miss Sinden notes, 'The figures . . . are no longer specimens chosen to demonstrate a specific thesis. . . .'[19] The protagonist, young Johannes Vockerat, though a believer in Darwin, Haeckel, and similar dangerous thinkers, has married a girl who shares the pious, orthodox views of his own parents. Into his 'exurban' house near Berlin, where he has retired to write—he hopes—a great book, an emancipated, 'new' woman, Anna Mahr, intrudes; like his wife Käthe, she is a finer person than he. Of course she 'speaks his language'; she is another potential 'saviour from afar.' He falls in love but, unable either to withstand the pressures exerted by his parents, his wife, and his Protestant conscience or to live without Anna, commits suicide.

The main characters are complex individuals; like most of the minor ones, they are convincingly drawn. Thus Käthe is limited, shy, rather lachrymose (she has recently borne a child and is exhausted; her husband's involuntary bullying has given her a sense of inferiority). Yet she is capable of real insight as well as of sweetness. A bit of an opportunist, Anna is basically decent, as well as intelligent and mature. Johannes is a worm—contrary no doubt to Hauptmann's intention—but just as such he is convincing. He is no more an intellectual than Alfred Loth was a true idealist; in both, one would guess, Hauptmann has unconsciously revealed his own limitations. A pseudo-scholar, Vockerat is equally a failure as husband, lover, and human being. Yet his 'well-meaning,' sanctimonious parents, almost unbearably *gemütlich* as long as their will is done, make one understand and even pity Johannes.

In Hauptmann's most famous and powerful play, *Die Weber* (1892), we no longer have even one foot in Ibsen's world. The subject, the revolt of the Silesian weavers of 1844, had taken place in Hauptmann's native province and affected his own family. Even in the Nineties, conditions were miserable, and Hauptmann implies clearly that the causes were remediable[20]—an implication that did not sit well with Wilhelm II or the governing classes generally. With all its misery, the atmosphere of *Die Weber* is far more bracing than that of *Einsame Menschen*. Here the 'saviour from afar'—the defiant soldier Jäger—has at least a fighting chance of success.

Usually it is maintained that the weavers as a group are the heroes of this broad historical canvas with its more than seventy characters. Doubtless this is sounder than focusing on the old pietist Hilse, who is killed by a stray bullet after refusing to take part in the revolt.[21]

Each of the five acts shows the tension rising. In the first, we learn that the rate for weaving has been lowered again, although the workers are literally starving. As their resentment and desperation increase, action replaces muttering; the looting in Act IV leads to an open battle in the last act: the Prussian soldiers are driven from the scene. Defying naturalist dogma, Hauptmann ends each act with a strong curtain. To draw the drama together, he has the 'Weavers' Song'—the 'Marseillaise of the proletariat'—mentioned or sung in every act. (Heine's powerful poem 'Die schlesischen Weber' was inspired by the same rebellion.)

Of course the audience knows that the revolt will be crushed. This, and the shift of focus to Hilse's death, has led some to claim that the play is without tendentiousness, a mere development of the *lacrimae rerum* theme. Obviously, though, Hauptmann's sympathies are clear, as is the implied demand for speedy reform.

Next to *Die Weber*, *Der Biberpelz* (1893) may well be Hauptmann's most rewarding play. His casting up accounts with the Prussian establishment, though kept in the comic mode, has the incisiveness his works too often lack. 'And he had reasons . . .': Wilhelm II, after the failure of his efforts to have *Die Weber* forbidden, had cancelled his box in the 'Deutsches Theater.' Hauptmann's revenge is splendid: his Wehrhahn (militant rooster!) is the Prussian at his worst—bullying, monocled, pseudo-military, thoroughly stupid. Hauptmann's protagonist, Frau Wolff, thoroughly amoral but determined that her family shall prosper, brilliantly bamboozles him. If only Hauptmann had used similar weapons against the Nazis!— Like *Einsame Menschen*, the comedy reflects the author's years in the semi-rural suburbs of Berlin.

In the same year Hauptmann published *Hanneles Himmelfahrt*, a drama less important in itself than as an indication of the new direction of his talent. In this study of a wretchedly mistreated, touching adolescent girl whose death is made euphoric by the visions of heaven accompanying it, everything can be rationally explained. Yet the accent lies not on its realistic side, but on the romantic and lyric; Hauptmann shifts effectively to very moving verse when Hannele imagines her ascension.

Thus *Hannele* is a portent of the new Hauptmann; but before turning to the neo-romantic mode the dramatist tried, in *Florian Geyer* (1895), to create a realistic historical drama—and, not incidentally—to rival Goethe, whose *Götz von Berlichingen* deals with the same theme, the Peasants War of the early sixteenth century. It was his most ambitious attempt, based on vast effort and industrious research,[22] and a catastrophic failure. While Hauptmann had so recently signally succeeded with an historical subject, his new theme was far vaster, and much farther from his own experience, than the Silesian revolt. Geyer and the peasant masses are the two sacrificial victims of this double tragedy; idealistic but rather inept, he is assassinated—no hero but a martyr. In part, perhaps, Hauptmann was ahead of his public; but reading this oversize drama today, one is reminded of Aristotle's dictum that a monster a thousand miles long cannot be beautiful.

The rejection of *Florian Geyer* so wounded Hauptmann that he devoted a symbolic drama to his defeat—*Die versunkene Glocke* (1896). In this verse tragedy, full of reminiscences of *Faust*, Silesian fairy tales, Fouqué's *Undine*, and other works, he appears as a bell-founder whose most ambitious creation falls and is ruined; he is torn between Christianity and paganism, and his private life is also unhappy. While Hauptmann wrote some effective realistic works in later years, such as his powerful tragedy *Rose Bernd* (1903), one suspects that he was never quite the same writer again. And surely his turning to symbol and myth had at least in part the character of escape. In any event, Hauptmann's partial but increasingly frequent defections from naturalism indicated that other literary forces were beginning to push that movement into the background.

Often it has been urged that naturalism is foreign to the German temperament, and the brevity of its reign would seem relevant evidence. Yet its impact is pervasive in German literature, as it is elsewhere: in the crasser aspects of expressionism, in the war novel, and in 'proletarian' fiction of the Twenties and Thirties, for example. The 'New Objectivity' of writers like Erich Kästner, some of

Brecht, and, with a difference, of Grass is a disillusioned naturalism. Even the 'blood and soil' school of Nazi writers was realistic compared to much that was written earlier about the peasants. Dated though even the best works of the movement are, it is worth remembering that the young Joyce admired the young Hauptmann. The German naturalists had an historic mission, as had their greater predecessors; however clumsily, they fulfilled it. Doubtless they were doctrinaire and often sentimental in setting down the truth as they saw it. Yet they were obsessed with truth, and their obsession was a noble one.

2 *Art . . . is not Nature:*
Neo-Romantic Tendencies

"Die Kunst heisst eben darum Kunst, weil sie nicht Natur ist."

—Goethe

'Art is called art precisely because it is not nature,' to translate the epigraph of this chapter. The real meaning of Goethe's apparently tautological remark is exemplified in the inevitable reaction against naturalism: the writers, mainly Viennese, who resisted Holz's well-meant precepts, believed passionately that the methods of the laboratory and the photographer's shop are not those of literature; that mimesis or representation is not copying; that art begins where the reducible ceases.

By the last decade of the nineteenth century radical changes were taking place in all areas of German cultural life. (This intellectual revolution was a highly international affair, which appears in literature primarily as the European symbolist movement and its outgrowths; but for the moment we must focus on the narrower scene.) In central Europe and in France, above all, a new romanticism affected and reshaped not only the arts but many aspects of philosophy, history, and psychology as well. Many enthusiasts felt that the age of positivism, materialism, and experimental science was ending. In some places and some fields, it was indeed; but of course the power and prestige of rational science, in its chosen realms, continued to expand, unchecked. The new movement stressed intuition, beauty, 'life' or 'soul' rather than 'mind' or 'reason.' Not surprisingly, its greatest achievements were in the arts.

The greatest ideals of the Nineties and of the turn of the century were beauty and life, both of which became veritable shibboleths. Understood polemically, as a challenge to the ugliness, dullness, and 'do-goodism' attributed to the naturalists, beauty was seen as an amoral or defiantly anti-moral value, to be upheld for its own sake alone. Thus Stefan George apostrophized 'das schöne Leben' and called for 'an art for art's sake,' a 'spiritual (*geistige*) art,' and pro-claimed his belief in 'a great renascence.'

The pupils of Hofmannsthal's dying artist in 'Der Tod des Tizian,' like the artists in Thomas Mann's *Fiorenza*, live for beauty alone. In the decorative arts and in stage settings the same note is struck. If one cannot achieve truly classic art, George's Algabal implies, then let it be dark, sinister, a *fleur du mal*: a 'dunkle grosse schwarze Blume.' From Baudelaire, Huysmans, and Wilde emanated a cult of the per-verse, the deliberately evil: Richard Strauss, D'Annunzio, Heinrich Mann, and even (briefly) Hofmannsthal paid tribute to it. Nothing can seem sillier to a century which has known true evil on the vastest scale than this self-conscious dabbling with wickedness.

Linked with the idea of beauty was that of life, as George's per-sonification of 'das schöne Leben' of course implies. Most briefly put, the new celebration of life implies that it is itself the highest of values and is to be judged by no other. Here Nietzsche is the great but by no means the only influence.* Writers as different as Dehmel, Rilke, and Wedekind assert repeatedly that to be intensely alive is what really matters. As a disavowal of petty moralizing and as a full-hearted acceptance, in the sense of Goethe's *Faust*, of the tragic aspect of life along with its others, this *Lebensphilosophie* has much to recommend it. Yet to hold that 'life' cannot be judged by any standard except itself invites not only anarchy (which may have its advantages) but the grossest barbarism. Many a fascist has been 'par-ticularly vital.' As a variation of the cult of life, the worship of youth—understandably widespread in the *Jugendbewegung*—made vitality largely a matter of chronology.

'Dialectically,' it is not surprising that the generation devoted to life was especially obsessed with the thought of death. Like the original romantics, the men of the Nineties were fascinated by death—'a great god of the soul' as Hofmannsthal called him. Death is almost omnipresent in neo-romantic literature, from Maeterlinck on. In large part, as in the mode of sinfulness, this cult represents a dilettantish playing with something one fears. Yet to regard life from the aspect of its ending may of course add a decisive dimension. *Respice finem!*

* See below, pp. 21–23.

In the 'sciences of the spirit' (*Geisteswissenschaften*), as the Germans call them, the revolt against positivism was almost as outspoken as it had been among the romantic practitioners of 'nature philosophy' around 1800. The emphasis was on intuiting the whole, *Wesensschau*, concentration on the gestalt, not the details. Nietzsche's interest in what he called monumental history fascinated many scholars. Again, aspects of the development which seem healthy to us today are inextricably mingled with very different ones.

Here we are faced with a paradox: many of the generation which proclaimed the value of intuition were sceptical about all knowledge —in drastic contrast to the 'real' romantics of a century before. Scepticism flourished particularly in Vienna, that most sophisticated of German-speaking cities, both in literature and philosophy.

> Wir wissen nichts von anderen, nichts von uns,
> Wir spielen immer, wer es weiss, ist klug—

says the wise Paracelsus, in Schnitzler's brief drama of that name. Only our sense perceptions have truth for us, the philosopher Ernst Mach taught. Conventions, dogmas, generalizations, bourgeois beliefs are generally false—here the new romantics agreed with their predecessors. But, where Fichte had claimed complete validity for his intuitions and Novalis found absolute truth revealed in dream, their successors were too sceptical (and sane?) for such flights of fancy. Dreams may mean the opposite of what they seem to imply, as Freud was not the only Viennese to realize.

Another Viennese, Hermann Bahr, argued ingeniously in 1891 that naturalism had destroyed itself: by precise observation the scientist found not three-dimensional objects but evanescent perceptions, sense impressions; hence impressionism was the order of the day.[1] Things were hardly that simple, but nerves and nervousness were indeed characteristic of the art, and the life, of the time. Robust scoffers even spoke of neuro-romanticism.

Certain themes and settings are especially characteristic of the period. Besides the artist figures, there are the aesthetes, who are generally presented much more coldly. In his early drama *Der Tor und der Tod* (1893), Hofmannsthal passed a severe though compassionate judgment on one of these fastidious, non-committed persons. Naturally this did not prevent critics from classifying the poet for years thereafter, usually with moral disapproval, as a mere aesthete. Schnitzler's 'playboys,' like Anatol, are artists or at worst dilettantes at life, like the faithless lover in *Liebelei*. In Thomas Mann's early, 'impressionistic' stories, near-artists, very minor writers, dilettantes, and plain failures afford evidence of his scepticism about his own profession.

Death and its advent is a theme characteristic of Maeterlinck, Hofmannsthal, and various minor writers. In the Christian tradition, death is the figure which brings tension and meaning to the *theatrum mundi*. In contrast Schnitzler, typically the scientist, shows in his novella 'Sterben' how the emotional erosion caused by a prolonged, hopeless illness can destroy the love of even a devoted woman for her doomed lover. Like Hauptmann, Schnitzler could work skilfully in either the naturalistic or neo-romantic mode, but his work, unlike the Silesian's, does not leave us with a sense of grave inconsistency: the integrity of his fine intelligence is preserved throughout. The literature of the Nineties often reflects, along with this concern about death and illness, the rising interest of the time in psychological conditions and techniques; Schnitzler uses hypnosis as a dramatic device in more than one of his works. And that life is a dream was a notion as familiar to Austrian audiences as to Spanish.

For the generation of the Nineties, certain ages and periods had a special nimbus. Above all, the Italian Renaissance seemed fascinating as the age of strong, ruthless, amoral aristocrats, as well as of beauty. C. F. Meyer's novellas, Burckhardt, and later Nietzsche reinforced a cult of the colourful and sinful Italians which went back at least to the Storm and Stress. Gobineau's dialogues, collected under the title *The Renaissance* (1877), established a link between aestheticism and racism; his follower, the naturalized German Houston Stewart Chamberlain, maintained that the Italian upper classes, being blond and blue-eyed, were Germanic.

Greek and medieval settings also appealed. While the Greeks may appear barbarous and almost psychotic, as in Hofmannsthal's *Elektra*, the Hellenic scene may be regarded more conventionally as idyllic, as in George's early poems. In the medieval sphere one tends to encounter Arthurian figures mainly notable for ill-starred love.

Like naturalism, neo-romanticism in Germany is representative of an international tendency which reached central Europe relatively

late. For George, Hofmannsthal, and Rilke, and still more so for
their successors, the influence of the French symbolist lyric is great.
George was particularly devoted to the poetry of Verlaine and
Mallarmé, both of whom he knew in Paris, as well as to Baudelaire's.

In the development of German drama, the late symbolic dramas
of Ibsen, Maeterlinck's plays of the 1890's, especially those concerned, like *The Blind* and *The Intruder*, with death, Wilde's *Salomé*,
and D'Annunzio's fiery if melodramatic pieces are significant.
Gesture, language rich in imagery and allusion—though it may,
like Maeterlinck's, be deliberately bare—and symbolic scenery take
the place of realistic conversation and detailed fidelity of stage
setting.

Incomparably the greatest influence on German literature from
the Nineties down to the Second World War was that of Nietzsche.
In force as well as direction, his impact is comparable to that of
Rousseau on the later eighteenth century. Largely neglected throughout the Eighties, Nietzsche's works began to attract attention after
he had gone mad. Notoriously, everyone has his own interpretation
of Nietzsche; scholars and critics differ as much as do certain writers.[2]
Inevitably; for he is as contradictory as he is stimulating. Of the
major German writers, he has demonstrably had a profound effect
on George, Thomas Mann, Benn, and probably Rilke; other figures,
Heinrich Mann, Wedekind, Dehmel, Morgenstern, and a swarm of
lesser men are in his debt—as were the original 'Youth Movement'
and some of its successors.

Nietzsche appeared to his readers as a great individualist, almost
an anarchist; as a critic and interpreter of culture generally; as the
discoverer of the Dionysiac element in life;[3] as the artist; as the
prophet (for the expressionists) of the 'new man.'* In the Twenties,
he was seen primarily as the Heraclitean philosopher who rejected
teleology, causality, and any sort of ideal in favour of the 'innocence
of the life process (*Unschuld des Werdens*)';[4] as the anti-prophet maintaining that 'God is dead'; later, as the John the Baptist of fascism;
and still more recently as one of the most dangerous of the ideologues
who led Germany astray. This last point is the burden of Thomas
Mann's essay 'Nietzsche in the Light of our Experience' (1946) but

* See below, p. 60.

it is safe to say that Nietzsche is still very much alive: the existentialists have claimed him as their own, as will others.

Without emphasizing chronology, it may be helpful to state Nietzsche's most seminal—or, in some cases, devastating—ideas, noting their relevance to literary developments. His early book *Die Geburt der Tragödie* (1872)—still perhaps his most appealing work—establishes the dichotomy between the Apollonian world of light, reason, and order and the Dionysian principle that life is tragic and is to be accepted as such. Apollo's is the beautiful world of appearance (*Schein*); Dionysus tries to overcome the dark tragedy of being through 'the ecstatic acceptance of the totality of life as the identity in all change.'[5] Obviously, the Dionysiac element is Schopenhauer's will, but Nietzsche reverses the 'life-denying' doctrine of his revered master and tells us to accept the will—which he later equated with will to power. Ostensibly beginning as a discussion of the Greek drama, *Die Geburt der Tragödie* soon appears as philosophy in its own right, and also in its less noble function as propaganda for Wagner's 'music dramas.' Agreeing as it does with the general rehabilitation of non-rational, vitalistic forces, the concept of the Dionysiac element had a great impact on creative writers, intellectuals, and the general climate of opinion.

Less profound is Nietzsche's well-known treatment of the 're-valuation of all values.' Christians and other ascetics, beginning with Socrates[!], he maintained, had agreed to call the aristocratic virtues —strength, courage, wealth, etc.—evil instead of good (*böse* rather than *gut*), whereas what was formerly considered poor and inferior (*schlecht*)—poverty, humility, weakness—was proclaimed good. While there is enough truth in this to make any Christian examine his own motives carefully, it hardly refutes either the New Testament or the Platonic Socrates. Some of the 'George circle' took it seriously, as did the fascist intellectuals.

A late after-effect of this 'slave revolt in morality,' Nietzsche held, was decadence and the emergence of 'the last man.' The latter comes from the world of humanitarianism, liberalism, socialism, and democracy (which Nietzsche shrilly condemned though he had never experienced it); with his petit-bourgeois evasion of tragedy, the last man finds life not worth living. Thus he is decadent; the hope for his contemporaries is that their own decadence can be overcome.

For him and for decadent society, as for Nietzsche himself, 'God is dead.' As Erich Heller has argued, this became one of Rilke's basic assumptions. Millions of others have shared it.

To offset his depressing caricature of the last man, Nietzsche invented the superman, that 'blond beast' who more or less resembles Cesare Borgia, Napoleon, Achilles, Goethe, etc., etc. This is perhaps the most pathetic existing instance of psychological compensation, but writers as different as George and Heinrich Mann played up the amoral and 'therefore' superhuman type. Heinrich's more perceptive brother, while praising Nietzsche's psychological penetration and even his cult of life, remarked that the blond beast and the superman embarrassed him; and he unmasked the 'blond and blue-eyed,' as being on the whole those rather dull, 'well adjusted' people, the burghers.

After 1945 it is hardly necessary to comment on the effects of Nietzsche's doctrines glorifying force and the military, or on the notion that 'a good war justifies any cause.' It is all too reminiscent of Oscar Wilde's flirtation with evil, and one can at best ignore it, without pretending, as some critics do, that Nietzsche 'didn't really mean it that way.' More important for literature is his belief[6] in the 'eternal return'—that all events take place again and again, or that, differently put, time is an illusion. Clearly, this notion is relevant to the reemergence of mythic patterns in modern literature.

Most important of all are Nietzsche's practice of proto-Freudian, 'unmasking' psychology—he regularly distinguished between overt and latent motivation—and his style. Undoubtedly he was one of the very few real stylists who wrote German prose between 1830 and 1890. To be sure, he can be uneven: *Also Sprach Zarathustra* reads like a parody of the New Testament today, or even like the works of Kahlil Gibran; and Nietzsche hardly deserves his own compliment that he was, with Heine, the greatest German master of prose. Yet he is never obscure; he avoids jargon and the endless arranging of clause within clause typical of the time; particularly in his middle years, he writes clearly, pointedly, wittily. Towards the end, his hyperbolic style, over-supplied with exclamation points and italics, often suggests hysteria.

To turn back to literature proper: Arthur Schnitzler, second only to Hofmannsthal among the Austrian writers of his generation, is one of the most underrated of German authors. There are several reasons: he was Jewish; his knowledge of depth psychology and honest treatment of sexual matters worried the inhibited; his wit could be mistaken for frivolity; his ironic objectivity was often interpreted as cynical nihilism. Like Wieland and Heine, he was penalized for his very intelligence. With some justification, critics have emphasized that Schnitzler's range is rather limited, and that his novellas and one-act plays are generally superior to his novels and full-length dramas. Above all, perhaps, interpreters have tended to avoid him because the lucidity of his writing often makes explication unnecessary.

In his objectivity and irony, and in his skill in rendering conversation of people of all levels, Schnitzler is comparable to Fontane, but the contrasts between the two are striking. While Fontane veered away from drastic scenes and 'shocking' subjects, Schnitzler tended to deal with extreme situations: death, sexual conflicts, neurotic and even psychotic states. He has been attacked for being obsessed with erotic matters; the truth is that he dealt courageously with a basic element of life which the Prussian novelist regarded as taboo. His urbanity was less serene than Fontane's; but how could any intelligent Jew feel serene in a milieu of virulent anti-Semitism? The Vienna of music and wine was also the city which shaped Hitler. After treating the general malaise affecting the relations between Christians and Jews in the novel *Der Weg ins Freie*, Schnitzler focused his drama *Professor Bernhardi* on a specific case involving racial and religious prejudice.

While he is usually listed, along with Hofmannsthal, Beer-Hofmann and a few others, as a member of the Vienna group, Schnitzler is far too authentic a writer to be pigeonholed. As Victor Oswald has pointed out,[7] Schnitzler was primarily a scientist; precisely as such, he could not believe that the naïve positivism of the Berlin naturalists compassed all truth. Thus *Anatol* (1893), a series of dramatic sketches illustrating the successes and failures of that amusing man-about-town, the 'hypochondriac of love,' and 'frivolous melancholiac,' as he calls himself, shows great awareness of the importance of unconscious states of mind. Anatol could easily discover through hypnosis whether his lady of the month has been faithful to him, but he is too astute to do so. (In Schnitzler's world, hardly anyone is faithful for long.) It would be easy to dismiss the characters of *Anatol* as mere butterflies—and I shall not in any case break them on a wheel—but their very wit reveals profound melancholy.

In his verses which served as a preface to *Anatol*, Hofmannsthal spoke of the 'comedy of our souls' and of formulating evil things attractively:

Böser Dinge hübsche Formel.

Schnitzler's *Reigen*, similar in technique to *Anatol*, neatly reduces the 'affair' to its most primitive element. Ten brief, incisive scenes show the endless shifts back and forth: lovers of all social classes are involved; the only constant is that everyone is inconstant. While certainly risqué in themselves, the episodes of *Reigen*, taken together, are anything but aphrodisiac, still less pornographic. The burden of the play would seem to be basically depressing: sexual drives are no respecters of personality; the characters involved have no more free will than Pavlov's dogs.

The complicated interworking of truth and falsehood fascinated Schnitzler particularly. Like *Paracelsus*, the brief drama *Der grüne Kakadu* turns on the play of reality and appearance, confounding them so ingeniously that the audience becomes as confused as do many of the characters. Two of his best novellas, 'Der blinde Geronimo' and 'Leutnant Gustl' (1901) have a similar purport. In the former, the blind beggar Geronimo disbelieves the words of his brother Carlo—who innocently caused his blindness, years before— as long as Carlo is telling the truth; but once he realizes that his brother has lied for him, he trusts him completely. Here, as often in his stories and plays, Schnitzler uses the technique of a sudden, drastic reversal. Similarly, Lieutenant Gustl was at the point of committing suicide when the civilian who knew the damning truth about him conveniently died at the eleventh hour. Most remarkable in 'Gustl' is its use, long before Joyce, of the stream-of-consciousness technique. The reader perceives everything through the mind—such as it is— of that utterly unpleasant fellow, Lieutenant Gustl. A quarter of a century later, Schnitzler used the same technique in his story 'Fräulein Else': a psychotic young girl gradually and unconsciously reveals the motives which lead her to disrobe in the lobby of a hotel.

It is impossible further to examine Schnitzler's work here. Suffice

3

it to say that he combined the naturalist's devotion to fact with the impressionist's interest in nuance; in other words, he told the truth. In a letter to Schnitzler,[8] Sigmund Freud implied that he hesitated to meet his fellow Viennese personally, being afraid of the writer's psychological insight and veracity. Freud's tone is jocular here, but he, perhaps better than anyone else, has taught us that many jokes must be taken seriously.

Hugo von Hofmannsthal appeared on the Viennese scene early in the Nineties; many thought that his poems, often signed with the pseudonym 'Loris,' were the finest lyrics since Goethe's; not without reason. For while Hofmannsthal never produced as challenging a work as the *Duineser Elegien*, the general level of his (few) poems is amazingly high: they are the most genuine lyrics to appear in German since Mörike's—at the least. The most memorable are products of his youth. When Hofmannsthal, after a severe psychological crisis, devoted himself largely to writing libretti for Richard Strauss and to establishing the Salzburg festival, the critics' cruelty was almost incredible. Thus Hermann Bahr, once an influential figure, wrote: 'I cannot forgive him for not having died at twenty; if he had, he could have been the most beautiful figure in world literature.' Disregarding such 'witticisms,' and surviving both private crisis and the liquidation of his beloved Austria, Hofmannsthal managed to write the subtlest comedy in the German language— *Der Schwierige*—and the impressive tragedy *Der Turm*.

Throughout his career Hofmannsthal wrote essays, mainly on literary topics but also on generally cultural and even political matters. Always a loyal Austrian, he became increasingly a good European as well. Extraordinarily widely read—indeed he was one of the most cultivated men of his time—he knew classical, English, French, and Italian literature.

The crisis which Hofmannsthal went through at the turn of the century threatened his very existence as a writer. After being hailed for a decade as the greatest literary genius writing in German, he became obsessed with the notion that words no longer had any meaning: communication was impossible. His eventual solution was the alliance with Richard Strauss: he hoped to find the answer in the union of word and music. Similarly, his efforts with Max Reinhardt and others to make Salzburg a great centre of music and

the drama were meant as a contribution to Western culture: to restore the artistic prestige of Austria and, above all, to assert the unity
of the European tradition.

Although even as perceptive a critic as Gundolf described
Hofmannsthal as a mere aesthete, this was only a potential danger:
few writers have combined his great sense of beauty with commitment to a moral point of view. Not only is his *Der Tor und der Tod*
an explicit warning against aestheticism; Hofmannsthal's 'Der
Kaiser und die Hexe,' another miniature drama, urges responsible
commitment and implicitly advises the reader not to embrace the
impressionist belief, which he had himself unforgettably expressed:

> Dass alles gleitet und vorübergeht.

That Heraclitean sense that everything is transitory is, to be sure,
one of the major themes of Hofmannsthal's early poetry, but it was
a mode of feeling which he was determined to overcome. Not that
he issues moral imperatives as George did; he had tact and a classic
sense of proportion and rightness. Thus the 'Ballade des äusseren
Lebens' gives the sense of the continuous stream of life, its beauty,
and yet its—and our—apparent lack of purpose. *Cui bono?*

> Was frommts, dergleichen viel gesehen haben?
> Und dennoch sagt der viel, der „Abend" sagt,
> Ein Wort, daraus Tiefsinn und Trauer rinnt
>
> Wie schwerer Honig aus den hohlen Waben.

There is then an inner life as well, and since like the 'heavy honey'
it is real, there is a meaning, however incomprehensible.—His triad
of poems in terza rima, 'Über Vergänglichkeit,' touches on similar
themes.

Probably Hofmannsthal's central poem is 'Weltgeheimnis,'
which expresses his view of the secret of poetry as well as of the
world, involving his idea of the human mind and his early belief in
'pre-existence,' which plays a part in many of his earlier works.*

* This last concept is Platonic: the tangible world is merely a copy of the
realm from which we come, 'trailing clouds of glory.' Lovers, youths, and
artists tend to linger in this original, supramundane world; but if a man is to
mature, he must forsake this Eden and enter the actual world around him.

The 'deep well' of the mind still remembers pre-existence; today, men have forgotten it, though a woman in love or a poet still has a dim sense of the lost secret.

Further, the ultimate secret lies encrusted and unseen in the words we use—

> So tritt des Bettlers Fuss den Kies,
> Der eines Edelsteins Verlies.

Like Rilke, George, Karl Kraus, and Morgenstern, to restrict our view to German literature, Hofmannsthal touches here on the worn, abraded state of language. How is one to reach the poetic symbol below the gray, gritty surface?[9]

In all there are less than a score of these early poems, some difficult like 'Lebenslied,' some as beautifully simple as 'Vorfrühling' or the love sonnet 'Die Beiden.' Hofmannsthal stated that he wished not to break the tradition of the lyric but to take it up again where Keats and Hölderlin had left it. In fact his lyrics, while far too clearly his own to be 'conventional,' are traditional in the best sense.

The best known of the several brief poetic dramas which Hofmannsthal wrote is *Der Tor und der Tod* (1893). Claudio, an aristocratic young aesthete, has lingered too long in the state of pre-existence; he can care for nothing but art and form. He himself complains that his life lacks all spontaneity:

> Ich hab mich so an Künstliches verloren,
> Dass ich die Sonne sah aus toten Augen
> Und nicht mehr hörte als durch tote Ohren:
> Stets schleppte ich den rätselhaften Fluch,
> Nie ganz bewusst, nie völlig unbewusst,
> Mit kleinem Leid und schaler Lust
> Mein Leben zu erleben wie ein Buch. . . .

Like some of Mann's early protagonists, Claudio is an elegant outsider. When Death confronts him, he protests that he has never lived; but that is exactly his offence. Returning from the dead, his mother, a young girl who loved him, and a friend then speak to him in turn—a use of the Dance of Death technique which Hofmannsthal was to repeat. Claudio has betrayed them all by never really committing himself to any of them.

Death, who has described himself as a beneficent deity—

> Ich bin nicht schauerlich, bin kein Gerippe!
> Aus des Dionysos, der Venus Sippe,
> Ein grosser Gott der Seele steht vor dir—

grants Claudio a moment of insight; faced with death, he has finally awakened to actuality. The irony of Death's final words—men always try to solve impossible riddles—prevents the ending from being too facile.

Written partly in four-beat *Knüttelvers* modelled on *Faust I*, partly in iambic pentameter, the verse is extraordinarily melodious and evocative. Greatly daring, Hofmannsthal took many words and turns of phrase from Goethe, as well as the metre, but the tone of his poetry is softer, gentler, one might say more Viennese. Hauptmann, in his borrowings for *Die versunkene Glocke*, was far less successful.

As Hofmannsthal's dramatic production was very large, I can only treat a representative group of his plays, without in any sense implying that the others are unimportant. *Elektra* (1903) reflects the black mood of the 'Chandos crisis' through which Hofmannsthal had been passing. When a writer says: 'Words fell to pieces in my mouth like mouldy mushrooms,' he is obviously not at his happiest; and Lord Chandos' fictitious letter to Francis Bacon, quoted here, undoubtedly expresses Hofmannsthal's own emotions. (Some twenty years later, Hemingway would make the same point, in somewhat earthier language.) Of course *Elektra* also owes a great deal to Wilde's *Salomé* and it may betray too great an accommodation with Richard Strauss, who was often eager to out-Wagner Wagner in producing big bangs. In any case, *Elektra* was a cathartic work for Hofmannsthal, who soon veered away from sensationalism and heavily accented 'decadence'—in other words, from what hostile critics called the 'Orientalism' of *Elektra*.

A bizarre but powerful mixture of ancient and modern, fifth-century Athens and turn-of-the-century Vienna, this *Elektra* is closer to Sophocles' version than to those of Aeschylus or Euripides. Hofmannsthal's heroine is equally fierce in her demand for bloody revenge; but where Sophocles' Elektra glories in her mission, the Austrian's protagonist collapses under its weight. At the same time, as a most friendly critic admits,[10] it is indebted to Nietzsche, Bachofen,

Hermann Bahr, and Freud. On the one hand, Hofmannsthal's intention of showing Elektra as a female Hamlet[11] must be respected, yet she is—to understate matters—half-crazy; *Elektra* is one of the 'one-act dramas of feminine hysteria,' like Kleist's *Penthesilea*, Strindberg's *Miss Julie*, and *Salomé*. One must not interrupt the action; for if the tension were broken, we would have leisure to regard these psychopathic young women with a colder eye.

Hofmannsthal's imagery, most uncharacteristically, suggests a pathological if not psychotic world. References to blood, scarlet, etc. determine the tone of the work. Snakes, dogs, carrion flies, corpses, caverns, and so on are typical symbols. For all her violence, Elektra impresses us, as Salomé does not, as a realized three-dimensional character. At the cost of her own fulfillment as a woman, she has devoted herself to killing the murderers of her all-too-loved father. Once they are slain, she has literally nothing more to live for; she dies, like Salomé, at the end of an ecstatic dance. The whole retinue of the guilty couple is killed, along with Aegisthus and Clytemnestra: vengeance is total. This sensational piece is hardly the result of seeing life steadily and seeing it whole, but no one will find it dull. Poetry, music, dance, and stage effects (also emphasizing blood and barbarism) are masterfully combined into a 'total work of art.'

The old German ideal of an all-embracing artistic structure (*Gesamtkunstwerk*) had been recently invoked by Richard Wagner, who tried to realize it in his enormously successful music dramas. For Hofmannsthal, the goal was rather the Mozartian *Gesamtkunstwerk*—after all, a very Austrian phenomenon. Strauss was far closer to Wagner than to Mozart, but in at least one admirable work, *Der Rosenkavalier*—the most brilliant operatic comedy since *The Marriage of Figaro*—the spirit of the earlier composer predominates.

Perhaps Hofmannsthal's despair about the effect of 'the word' was the primary reason for his turning to the opera, but he had more positive grounds also. In an essay of 1929 he wrote:

> If the present is anything, it is mythic—I know no other word for an existence which is acted out before such immense horizons —for the state of living surrounded by millenia, for the way that the Orient and the Occident flow into our consciousness. . . . It is impossible to catch the sense of this in dialogues on a middle-class

level. Let's create mythological operas. That is the truest of all forms.[12]

This statement comes late; and a critic could object that the finest of the Hofmannsthal-Strauss operas are not mythological; but he would be wrong. Why would the Marschallin in *Der Rosenkavalier* have the name 'Marie Theres',' unless she were a reflection of the beloved empress, and thus of some archetypal mother? What could be more typical than the silver rose which Octavian gives to his intended wife? In line with this mythopoetic aim, Hofmannsthal and Strauss presented, in their more successful works, genuine gestalten, not 'mouthpieces of philosophical ideas,' like Wagner's Wotan.

Of course the comic side of *Der Rosenkavalier* is at least as important as the mythic. Like many of Hofmannsthal's works it is set in the Rococo period and plays in a stylized Vienna—the Vienna of Canaletto as he called it elsewhere, a city marked by more wit, gaiety, charm, and musicality than ever existed even in *Austria felix*. The characters speak a language of Hofmannsthal's own invention, 'a mixture of Viennese dialect, the jargon spoken by the nobles, and Rococo grammar.'[13] Just as the action ranges from potential tragedy through various levels of comedy to sheer farce, the spectrum of characters extends from the ageing Marschallin—who meets the necessity of renouncing her young lover with dignity and grace—to the boorish womanizer Baron Ochs von Lerchenau. Like Da Ponte's *Figaro* the text of *Der Rosenkavalier* would be excellent comedy in itself; but it would be unthinkably barbarous to waste the music.

Based on an incident in Casanova's *Memoirs*, *Cristinas Heimreise* is also set in the eighteenth century and located in Venice, a city Hofmannsthal found enchanting. The lovely and innocent Cristina is desired both by the seducer Florindo and by his friend, a sea-captain. While she is unable to resist Florindo, Cristina morally survives her 'fall'; at the end, the drama implies that she will marry the worthy captain. As the Casanova of the piece, Florindo appears not as a villain but an erotic virtuoso, a type of aesthete; the more mature captain is the ethical man. Increasingly Hofmannsthal writes of the individual's relations to others; his stress on the 'I-Thou' link recalls Martin Buber. To marry is to commit oneself, to build a bridge not only to another person, but to society—a theme joining the short early play 'Der Kaiser und die Hexe' to his subtlest comedy, *Der Schwierige* (1921).* While Hofmannsthal's emphasis on moral matters is very explicit at times, it is never pharisaical nor puritanical.

Based on the morality play *Everyman*, *Jedermann* has become world famous through its performances at the Salzburg festival, where it is normally repeated each summer. In writing the work, Hofmannsthal kept the Salzburg scene in mind, admirably adapting his stage effects to that Baroque city. In his version, Everyman is an average person, sinful but no villain, who is led by Good Works to find the way to repentance and finally obtains grace. If the play has become a tourist's attraction—a cliché rather than a religious experience—nothing was farther from Hofmannsthal's intentions.

In a brilliant article,[14] Professor Alewyn has shown how Hofmannsthal transcended the ideal of 'das schöne Leben.' One must grow out of the trance of 'pre-existence,' for precisely by turning his back on ordinary reality, a man will make it, as Wilde did, something very ugly indeed.

Richard Beer-Hofmann (1866–1945), a close friend of Hofmannsthal's, shared the flair for psychology, the preoccupation with death, the sense that everything is in flux, and the interest in the theatre characteristic of Viennese writers around the turn of the century. The quality that most sets him apart from them is his devotion to the Jewish tradition, the mingled pride and humility he felt as one of the 'people of the Covenant.'

While Beer-Hofmann first made his mark with the publication of his very tender 'Schlaflied für Mirjam' in 1898, his long novella *Der Tod Georgs*, published in 1900, is his most interesting early work. Thematically, the story is remarkable mainly for its morbidity: the narrator relates not only the premature death of his gifted friend Georg but the protracted, fatal illness of a completely imaginary woman; the work is far more 'obsessed with death' than is Schnitzler's *Sterben* or any of Hofmannsthal's early plays. In technique however it is remarkable: it is an interior monologue of over 200 pages, in which the reader is continually inside the mind of the aesthetically sensitive (and extraordinarily neurotic) narrator Paul. He is 'neuro-romantic' in the extreme, devoted to nuances, longings,

* See pp. 112–114 for Hofmannsthal's late works.

and muted passion; but at the end, he derives a certain strength from his awareness of Jewish tradition.

It was Beer-Hofmann's great ambition to celebrate that tradition in a trilogy of plays devoted to the Biblical David, but he was able to complete only the prologue, *Jaákobs Traum* (1918),* *Der junge David* (1933),* and a 'Vorspiel auf dem Theater zu König David.' *Jaákobs Traum* is traditional in style: written in melodious, lucent blank verse, it contains reminiscences of *Faust* and of *Iphigenie auf Tauris*. (Beer-Hofmann, one of the greatest directors of the *Burgtheater*, had supervised brilliant performances of both these plays.) In theme it stresses the burden which the divine blessing implies— a burden which Mann's charismatic Joseph was found unworthy to sustain. On a similarly lofty plane, *Der junge David* treats the conflict between David's loyalty to Saul and that to Israel as a whole. Jewish patriotism is sharply distinguished from racism. Unfortunately this stylistically attractive if over-lengthy play is more epic than dramatic. Beer-Hofmann's earlier drama *Der Graf von Charolais* (1904) was one of the great stage successes of neo-romanticism but has slight intrinsic interest. Like Hofmannsthal, though less successfully, Beer-Hofmann laboured to renew the great traditions of Austrian drama.

Although readers today tend to the conviction that much neo-romantic literature is irresponsibly subjective, a luxury for the leisured classes, the Austrian writers of the period, at their best, transcended the mode of their time and created works of enduring value. Further, their stress on the inner life provided a useful counterweight to the scientism of the naturalistic school.

* From an Austrian, and above all from a Jewish point of view, the irony of these dates is tragic indeed.

3 *The Rebirth of the German Lyric*

"Der Nachtigallen, der sind viel."

—*Gottfried von Strassburg*

Along with Hofmannsthal and Rilke, Stefan George is rightly regarded as one of the three great poets who reshaped German lyric poetry after the period of the epigones. There was a great plenty of other poets (and versifiers) around; some of them, like Richard Dehmel, were once renowned: several swollen reputations have been deflated. Also, there were charming minor writers like Richard Beer-Hofmann or the delightfully witty Christian Morgenstern; but George and Rilke were the men who really brought the new poetry to Germany. (Hofmannsthal, after all, was a renovator rather than an innovator.)

As in the fine arts, 'the word' came primarily from Paris, and George was the first creative writer to hear it and then to speak in the new symbolist manner. Like naturalism, symbolism reached central Europe very late. As an unknown young man of twenty-one, George was fortunate enough to meet the new French poets in Paris and was admitted to Mallarmé's soirées. Up to this time his own verse had been conventional. Suddenly transformed, he invented a *lingua romana* of his own—he was a linguistic genius—and he wrote poems in it which he then translated into German.[1] These, while marking a great step in his development, are not in themselves remarkable. Soon, however, he wrote genuinely symbolist verses like those in *Algabal*, highly wrought, formally perfect. He referred to his immediate predecessors in the German lyric as 'lambs'—innocent and stupid.

On a small scale, George's radical change of the physical appearance of a printed page parallels the revolution in his style. He gave up capitalizing nouns, introduced a new punctuation, a unique, unmistakable type face, and insisted on using heavy, elegant paper. The artist Melchior Lechter, a belated German analogue to William

Morris, was responsible for making the decorations, covers, and title pages equally 'Georgean.'

For good though not aesthetic reasons, George is the least liked today of the three major poets who emerged in the Nineties. His arrogance, the dictatorship he exerted over his 'circle'—alas, the writer as *Führer* is a familiar German figure—his intransigent nationalism in the Twenties are all relevant. When George proclaimed that the youthful minor poet Maximilian Kronberger was literally a god, he revealed a fervid fanaticism, to use no stronger word, which cannot be dismissed as a mere whim of genius. While George's pronunciamentos and poses, especially during his later career, do not vitiate his poetry, they cast a lurid light on his pretensions as prophet.

In contrast, the young George was so internationally oriented that he ended an important poem with a line from the *Chanson de Roland*:

Returnent Franc en France dulce terre.

And, though his political stance, from 1914 on, was ambiguous or worse, he left Nazi Germany voluntarily, refused the presidency of the German Academy offered him by Goebbels, and made clear in his will that his body was to be buried in Switzerland, and to remain there. '*Si monumentum requiris. . . .*'

One can best approach George's first important cycle of poems, *Algabal* (1892), through reading his short poem 'Die Spange,' which appeared the preceding year at the close of the brief volume *Pilgerfahrten*:

> Ich wollte sie aus kühlem eisen
> Und wie ein glatter fester streif.
> Doch war im schacht auf allen gleisen
> So kein metall zum gusse reif.
>
> Nun aber soll sie also sein:
> Wie eine grosse fremde dolde. . . .

Since no medium exists from which the poet can form classic verse, he will aim at the baroque richness of red gold and flashing jewels. Dedicated to the memory of that unhappy, half-mad aesthete Ludwig II of Bavaria, *Algabal* is on one level an evocation of the decadent, bloodthirsty Emperor Heliogabalus, just the type to appeal to a Wilde or a Beardsley; but actually Algabal is the poet himself, creating an underground realm of artifice deliberately repellent to the Philistine:

> Mein garten bedarf nicht luft und nicht wärme,
> Der garten den ich mir selber erbaut
> Und seiner vögel leblose schwärme
> Haben noch nie einen frühling geschaut.

How, he asks at the end, can he create a 'dunkle grosse schwarze blume'—the dark flower of art? (The 'blue flower' of romanticism had come to seem banal.) It is typical that the key poems of the cycle deal with poetry itself; symbolistic writers tend more than others to make art their subject. Thus 'Vogelschau,' the last poem of *Algabal*, augurs a new style: the hot wind in which the white swallows hover changes to 'cold and clear,' recalling the 'cool iron' of 'Die Spange.'

George's next important cycle, *Das Jahr der Seele*, takes its title from a confident, affirmative line of Hölderlin,[2] but its mood is one of quiet melancholy. Significantly, the year of the soul contains no spring: the decisive season is autumn; parting and resignation are the basic motifs. Some lines convey a frightening sense of rejection and nothingness:

> Nun heb ich wieder meine leeren augen
> Und in die leere nacht die leeren hände.

On one level, the poems tell of two lovers who must separate, but the preface warns that, to an unusual degree, 'I' and 'Thou' are the same spirit. Nature is reflected in the soul and vice versa; while nature has been subjected to discipline, appearing as a park inhabited by swans, unhappy lovers, and a handsome youth, we are at least no longer in Algabal's airless realm. The ordinary reader could feel somewhat at home, and the book had great popular success.[3] Its most famous poem shows George's strength and his weakness. It begins:

> Komm in den totgesagten park und schau:
> Der schimmer ferner lächelnder gestade·
> Der reinen wolken unverhofftes blau
> Erhellt die weiher und die bunten pfade.

The unexpected beauty of autumn is unforgettably evoked: the park has only been *called* dead; the colour of the sky is 'unhoped for.' A bit later, however, the poem tells us to select and 'kiss' the late roses —surely, to quote *Patience*, this is too utterly utter.

Der Teppich des Lebens, another major work, consists of seventy-two poems, each of sixteen lines; rhyme generally prevails. As in *Der Stern des Bundes* and elsewhere, George organizes his poems according to a strictly mathematical pattern. It is equally characteristic that the title contains a master image which controls the whole cycle. Among the major themes are the aesthetic life; the élite, devoted to the ideal of Greece; symbolism in art; a new sense of 'the Volk' and the national past (as in the powerful poem 'Urlandschaft'); the absolute devotion of a follower to his leader; and the Dionysiac experience conveyed in 'Traum und Tod.' The last word of the cycle, like the last word in Mann's *Der Tod in Venedig*, is 'death':

> Glanz und ruhm rausch und qual traum und tod.

But George was becoming increasingly a prophet with definite dogmas to proclaim. 'Rausch und qual' do not disappear from his work, but the lyric 'charge' diminishes.

George was almost as important as a cultural guide as in his role as poet. While his journal *Blätter für die Kunst* (1892–1919) was deliberately directed at a small elite, it had great influence. International in its choice of contributors, it stood at first for art for beauty's sake, for symbolism against naturalism. As George increasingly aspired, with some success, to play the part of *praeceptor Germaniae*, the tone of the *Blätter für die Kunst* changed accordingly.

Something imperious in the poet's personality made him, for better and for worse, a leader of men. In the over forty years of his cultural career he attracted many of the most brilliant German intellectuals and scholars—Gundolf, the critic Max Kommerell, Norbert von Hellingrath (a leading 'rediscoverer' of Hölderlin), the poet Karl Wolfskehl, and others. At the same time, he acted as a magnet for dubious literati, for not ungifted doctrinaires who were more than a little mad—the anti-rationalist and 'graphologist' Klages, the anti-Semite Schuler, the poet Derleth, whose proclamations demanded a synthesis of Christianity and fanatic militarism.[4] The ambiguity of the George-circle is typical of much German culture at that time, fascinating but frightening, brilliantly unbalanced—in a word, Nietzschean.

Around 1903, George's following was diminished by a schism; the extreme anti-rationalist wing, the 'Cosmics' [*sic*!], left him. Possibly because of an unconscious need to outbid them, George became convinced that the youthful poet Maximilian Kronberger, with whom he fell in love the following year, was God, or at least a god. George's loyal followers accepted this claim, and became still more fanatic in their devotion: his circle became a rigid hierarchy. While 'it is difficult not to write a satire' about the whole group, one must state that some of his poems to Maximin, as he called him, are among his finest.

George's longest book of poetry, *Der siebente Ring* (1907), is a massive volume consisting of seven symmetrically arranged cycles. The first deals like the seventh with the poet's own time; the second and sixth are focused mainly on personalities and their interrelations; the third and fifth on irrationality and passion. At the apex is the cycle 'Maximin,' which aims at nothing less than presenting George's 'Beatrice' as a god. Here, as in George's next book *Der Stern des Bundes*, the central image is that of concentric circles or rings surrounding a flame or star. This metaphor stresses not only the centrality of Maximin; it is an image of the closely integrated union or *Bund* of devoted followers, hierarchically arranged around George himself. He in turn is only the John the Baptist of the divine youth, who had died three years before, saving the *Bund* from having an embarrassingly human, ageing god on its hands.

There is a close connection between George's league of men and youths devoted to reorganizing the entire cultural life of the time[5] and the 'leagues of young men' (*Männerbünder*) which sprang up after 1918, with the aim of reorganizing the German state and then reversing the result of the First World War.[6] Not that George's circle consisted primarily of proto-fascists or madmen—though it included both; it is the demand for dominance, indeed for dictatorship, which links it to political totalitarianism. Only a member of a *Männerbund*, a poem in the second cycle states, can discipline and control nature—*die grosse Nährerin*—a fertile but regrettably female entity.

In the central cycle, George celebrates Maximin with a wealth of imagery, largely of Christian origin. However bizarre, these poems do reflect a fervent emotion. The rest of *Der siebente Ring* is mainly notable for showing us George the prophet: though he feels himself a 'humble slave' of Maximin, he is omniscient and infallible *vis-à-vis* mortals. In the last triumphant poem, George declares that he is eager for new things—'zu jeder neuen Fahrt bereit'—a surprisingly open-minded attitude.

Yet the form of *Der Stern des Bundes*, even tauter than that of its predecessor, is as severe as the poet's increasingly authoritarian attitude. A hundred poems, all brief and compact, are divided according to a strict pattern. (More and more, George felt himself, apparently, a sort of neo-pagan Dante.) The guest of Mallarmé has become a nationalist using phrases like 'the holy youth of our folk,' and foretelling, like the expressionists whom he abhorred, that a great cataclysm, a Holy War, would come. Technically the verses of *Der Stern des Bundes* are admirable but the lyric note recedes: George seems to have sold his birthright for a mess of 'prophetic' pottage.

Thus it comes as no surprise that George did not publish another book of poetry until 1928, when his last, *Das neue Reich*, appeared. Here too the tone is peremptory, the prophet's attitude—George is no longer primarily the poet—ambiguous. His long polemical poem 'Der Krieg' castigates the meretricious regime of Wilhelm II and well proclaims the death of 'the old god of battles,' only to end with an equally meretricious declaration of a unique link between the two great classic peoples, the ancient Greeks and the contemporary Germans; and the clear implication that Germany will be the 'lord of the future.' At the very close of *Das neue Reich*, however, a love poem re-achieves the lyric note:

> Du blühend reis vom edlen stamme
> Du wie ein quell geheim und schlicht
> Du schlank und rein wie eine flamme
> Du wie der morgen zart und licht.

Yet basically one feels that while George did at his best speak with the tongues of men and of angels, he had not love. While his role in twentieth-century German literature is a major one, it is by no means attractive.

George was a gifted and productive translator, drawing on the literature of many countries. At times, to be sure, he imposes his own stiff solemnity on poems of a very different sort, as in his rendering of Shakespeare's sonnets. He is at his best with sections of the *Divine Comedy*. He translated most of Baudelaire's *Fleurs du Mal* and various other French and English poets of the nineteenth century. Perhaps the most important of his achievements was the introduction of a new seriousness towards poetry and the poet.

While neither George's personality nor his poems were such as to attract a large following, Rainer Maria Rilke (1875–1926) became probably the most widely read German poet since Heine; one can speak of adoration in many instances. As frequently happens, many of his popular verses do not rank among his best: thus his early exaltations of poverty, of the Almighty, or his account of the last crowded hours of Cornet Christoph Rilke tend to be 'sweet' and at times unconvincing. Conversely his great *Duineser Elegien*, like *Die Sonette an Orpheus*, are almost as difficult as they are rewarding. The most accessible of his best work, the two volumes entitled *Neue Gedichte*, speak to any sensitive reader.

A genius in the full sense of the word, Rilke experienced periods of inspiration in which whole series of poems poured forth almost without pause. (There were also barren times, when he often concentrated *faute de mieux* on translating; like Hofmannsthal and George, he was successful and versatile in this.) A useful key to understanding Rilke lies in his belief that we must transform raw experience into works of art, imparting to it a kind of reality which mere life does not have, somewhat as Cézanne transformed three-dimensional apples into lasting entities. Elsewhere Rilke said that the only real world lies within, in the *Weltinnenraum*; of course the paradox is that the artist must make this internal world accessible to others.

No prophet, philosopher, nor guide to life, Rilke nevertheless expressed flashes of extraordinary wisdom in his poems. Thus one of them tells us that real growth comes not from a series of victories, which may then inhibit one's freedom; rather

> . . . sein Wachstum heisst, der Stetsbesiegte
> von immer Grösserem zu sein.

Rilke's belief in emotional isolation, in love as the preserver of the distance between two people, expresses an aspect of the truth but hardly the central one. In his cult of the unloved lover—to *be* loved is banal and somehow deleterious to the person loved—he rationalized his own inability to maintain a close relationship for long. At first his pre-occupation with death appears as simply the usual neo-romantic fascination, but he developed the provocative notion of a death of one's own—*der eigene Tod*—which grows organically from a man's own character and experiences; this is the proper end of life, whereas an 'alien death,' forced on him by another or by chance, is horrible.

Rilke's childhood and youth could hardly have been less auspicious. Frail, he was dressed as a girl by his neurotic mother until he was five; at ten, sent to the opposite extreme, a military academy; then for a while to a business school; somehow he survived to attend various universities. From his early days, writing was a consolation; and like many other seemingly labile people, he had hidden strength.

Rilke himself had no high opinion of his early verses, which are indeed facile, often sentimental. Although *Das Buch der Bilder* and especially *Das Stunden-Buch* still reveal a certain modish softness, a new note appears, as in the admirable 'Herbsttag' and 'Pont du Carrousel' of the former collection. In the latter work, however, the poet flirts coyly with his 'neighbour' God, around whom he 'circles.' The third section of *Das Stunden-Buch*, devoted to asceticism, poverty, and death, shows many touches of genius, but is still marked by an occasional insincerity: its low point is the notorious line—

> Denn Armut ist ein grosser Glanz aus Innen—

which inspired one of Georg Grosz's harshest caricatures. Yet in the same book are found two lines which express the *fin-de-siècle* mood unforgettably:

> Die Könige der Welt sind alt
> Und werden keine Erben haben.

The uncertainty of tone is typical: despite a variety of experiences— wide travels, love affairs, notably one with that remarkable blue-stocking Lou Andreas-Salomé, the experience of Russia and of two visits to Tolstoy, and most recently marriage and fatherhood—

Rilke still seems the brilliant apprentice. Not until he went to Paris in 1902 to write a monograph on Auguste Rodin was Rilke clearly assured of a breakthrough; even collections published well after this time are uneven. With the *Neue Gedichte* (1907–08) the great Rilke emerges. Deeply indebted to Cézanne and Rodin—he became the latter's secretary—he evolved the notion of a *Dinggedicht*—a poem evoking an object, work of art, animal, or human being with the greatest possible concreteness and palpability. Such an approach saves one from the vagueness and insincerity of undisciplined emotions and imperfectly sensed ideas—the worst faults of Rilke's earlier verse.

Thus '*Dinggedicht*' is a deliberately one-sided term: Rilke needed to make his own poetry more 'thingish.' He never forgot that the 'thing' has to be transformed within the poet—'We are the bees of the invisible'—into an 'art-thing.' In other words, the *Dinggedicht*, as Bernhard Blume has proved conclusively,[7] is a symbolic poem, not just 'any old thing' presented for its own sake. The greatest of the *Neue Gedichte* imply something far beyond themselves. If the 'Archaischer Torso Apolls' is the most nakedly explicit—

> Du musst dein Leben ändern—

'Der Panther' and 'Das Karussell' also make a moral statement. 'Spanische Tänzerin,' perhaps the most brilliant lyric in all this two-volume collection, is mainly concerned, as a typical symbolistic poem, with the function of the artist. While even in the *Neue Gedichte* a certain artiness remains—coyness about religion, occasional chichi rhymes—these are the works of a great poet.

Of the special characteristics of Rilke's poetry of this period, the 'big line,' especially sententious and memorable, is one of the most noteworthy. Usually it stands at the end of a poem, or is set off by the rhyme scheme, or both. Often it contains a striking image and/or an epigrammatic turn. A few examples, aside from the ending of 'Archaischer Torso' quoted above, follow:

> stand, wie Turme stehen, ihr Gebet.

Or, at the end of 'Der Auszug des verlorenen Sohnes':

> Ist das der Eingang eines neuen Lebens?

The effect may be sinister, like the last line of 'Die Kurtisane':

> gehn wie an Gift an meinem Mund zugrund—

or playful, as in 'Das Karussell':

> Und dann und wann ein weisser Elefant.

There are dozens of other instances. Rilke's virtuosity in the use of alliteration, enjambment, interior rhyme, unexpected end rhyme, etc. needs only to be mentioned.

Rilke's *Werther* is his novel *Die Aufzeichnungen des Malte Laurids Brigge* (1910): his protagonist Brigge endures the fate which might have been Rilke's if he had not met Rodin. Much more than *Werther*, *Brigge* is an amalgam of personal experience (*Angst* and death in Paris) and literary emulation: the protagonist's aristocratic Danish background derives from Jens Peter Jacobsen. Themes familiar from the poems appear: women lovers are far superior to their male counterparts; a man needs 'his own death'; it is best not to be loved. At the most, God might love Brigge, 'but not yet.' The book's emphasis, almost expressionistic in its shrillness, on the hideousness of great cities, on epileptics, madmen, hospitals, etc., contrasts harshly with its account of the Danish landed aristocracy; but no social criticism is implied. Few would pretend that *Malte Laurids Brigge* is great fiction, but it gives valuable insight into the spirit of the time, and of its author.

Carried away like most of his countrymen by enthusiasm for the war, Rilke wrote his uncharacteristically martial 'Fünf Gesänge' in 1914; a year later a series of extremely explicit poems on the pleasures of sex. He was released from military service after a brief term, but suffered keenly in the atmosphere of war. Like George, Mann, and many others he wrote little of high literary value during these dreadful years.

Around 1900, many observers ranked Richard Dehmel (1863–1920) with the most important masters of the German lyric. Today his importance seems mainly historical: his poems show the impact of both Nietzschean individualism and socialistic sympathy with the worker; their style reflects the naturalistic dogma that the 'facts of life,' whether social or sexual, must be honestly recorded. Dehmel, however, rejected naturalism as such. Indeed, his beliefs were anything but consistent: he championed the ruthless individual and the masses, internationalism and patriotism (he voluntarily enlisted in the German army at fifty-one), celebration of life and Schopenhauerian pessimism. Yet there is value in the honesty with which he expressed these tensions, all of them typical of German culture at his time.

Although Dehmel published dramas, a diary of his experiences during the war, and even children's books, only his verse had a major effect on his age. His early poems show a debt to Goethe, Schiller, Lenau, and Heine.[8] Later, he occasionally wrote in the impressionistic manner of his friend Liliencron, and learned from French poets like Verlaine, whose 'La lune blanche luit dans les bois' he translated.

Dehmel's major lyric theme is sexual love, as the title of such volumes as *Aber die Liebe* (1893), *Weib und Welt* and *Zwei Menschen*—a novel in verse—indicate. In the cycle 'Verwandlungen der Venus'* he presents numerous aspects of the goddess, ranging from 'Venus Vulgivaga' to 'Venus Urania.' While outspoken, these poems are too serious to be pornographic and generally too wordy to be effective.

A second major concern of Dehmel's was that with Weltanschauung and morality. While he rejected Nietzsche's concepts of 'master morality' and the superman, he echoed the philosopher's acceptance of life as a struggle, his rehabilitation of the senses, and his adjuration to 'become the one you really are.' Typically, one of Dehmel's central poems is called 'Selbstzucht,' and he ended another:

> und sollst dich mühn von Herz zu Herz
> aus dumpfer Sucht zu lichter Glut!

By no means a Marxist,[9] Dehmel was keenly aware of the 'social problem.' One of his lyrics recounts the death of an infant in a fourth-class railway carriage; another, 'Der Arbeitsmann,' was famous as an expression of social sympathy.

Not surprisingly, he was often at his best in his least ambitious, non-hortatory verse; as in the brief, impressionistic 'Stimme des Abends,' which begins

> Die Flur will ruhn.
> In Halmen, Zweigen
> ein leises Neigen.

* First published in *Aber die Liebe*.

Extraordinarily uneven, Dehmel was capable of writing, in a love-poem: 'Zwanzigtausend Schafe schauen/immer wieder nach dir hin.' Appealing though his sincerity often is, he rarely transmuted his experiences into genuinely poetic language, seldom transcended autobiographical or didactic statement.

Relatively unknown during his life, Max Dauthendey (1867–1918) gained posthumous fame in the Twenties, mainly for his lyrics and his volume of novellas, *Die acht Gesichter am Biwasee* (1911). He also wrote two novels, other collections of shorter fiction, dramas, and even a book an aesthetics (in Swedish).

Dauthendey's Weltanschauung is a very eccentric one, but it casts some light on his verse. It is highly eclectic, deriving in part from Nietzsche but largely from ideas transmitted to him by his friends and professors. One of his central beliefs was the cult of *Weltfest-lichkeit*: life, even when painful, is festive and must be celebrated. His moods are normally expressed by a key colour, used as a leit-motif. (A painter, he was obsessed by colour throughout his life.) His first volume of poems is entitled *Ultra Violett* (1893). Further, he thought that the universe is made up of sentient atoms, somewhat reminiscent of Leibniz' monads. Even stones consist of atoms which feel love and hate: the psyche is everywhere. Further, he believed that in the correspondences between sound and colour the key to the universe could be found.[10]

A 'colour-intoxicated man.' Dauthendey had the ideal tempera-ment for an impressionist. As many of his poems and prose descrip-tions show, one can apply the term to him without straining the analogy to painting. His impressionism is evident in the brief lyric beginning—

> Winde quälen die Bäume,
> Die Blätter frieren und gilben—

and equally in 'Rosenduft,' with its very bold use of synaesthesia:

> Weinrot brennen Gewitterwinde,
> Purpurblau der Seerand.
> Hyancinthentief die ferne Küste.
>
> Ein Regenbogen, veilchenschwül,
> Schmilzt durch weihrauchblaue Abendwolken.

Im Taudunkel lacht
Eine heisse Nachtigall.

An inveterate traveller, Dauthendey delighted in evoking exotic scenes. He was particularly fascinated by the Orient, as his collections of 'Asiatic novellas,' *Lingam* and *Die acht Gesichter am Biwasee*, bear witness, and as do many of his poems. When the war of 1914 broke out, Dauthendey was in the Far East; unable to return to Germany, he spent the last four years of his life in Java and Sumatra.

With Erich Kästner,* Christian Morgenstern (1871–1914) is the leading writer of humorous verse in recent German letters. While Kästner should not be dismissed as superficial, he addresses himself to immediate social, political, and moral questions. Morgenstern is a subtle critic of the human mind, especially as it appears in language. Much indebted to the linguistic philosophy of Fritz Mauthner,† Morgenstern comments wittily on the arbitrary way we assign names to things, stressing that words may keep us from 'things-in-themselves' and that they often precede or distort the objects signified.[11] Thus a word like 'knee' makes sense only in the context of a larger physical unit; the poet writes:

Ein Knie geht einsam durch die Welt.
Es ist ein Knie, sonst nichts!

What happens to a lattice fence, he asks, if the space between the individual slats is removed? In 'Fisches Nachtgesang' he illuminates the problem of non-verbal communication by producing a diagram of symmetrically arranged symbols of long and short feet. A brief poem illustrates the attitude of the aesthete:

Wenn ich sitze, will ich nicht
sitzen, wie mein Sitz-Fleisch möchte,
sondern wie mein Sitz-Geist sich,
sässe er, den Stuhl sich flöchte. . . .

Like Kraus, Morgenstern often uses the pun to make a serious point.

Morgenstern underrated his light verse. Philosophically inclined, he wrote poems to express a Nietzschean view of the world by a

* See below, p. 103.
† See esp. Mauthner's *Beiträge zu einer Kritik der Sprache* (1901–02) and *Die Sprache* (1907).

myth of his own, as in the volume *In Phanta's Schloss* (1895), or to celebrate love, as in *Ich und Du*. Influenced by the anthroposophist Rudolf Steiner, he embraced a highly spiritualistic Christianity in his last years. Like Dehmel, he was most successful in brief impressionistic poems without metaphysical ambitions. Although his serious lyrics show genuine feeling, he found his own idiom primarily in the humorous, sometimes grotesquely fantastic verses of *Galgenlieder* (1905), *Palmström* (1910), and other brief volumes; the collection *Alle Galgenlieder* contains them all.

4   *The Major Novelists, 1900-1918*

Und dichten, Gerichtstag halten
Über das eigene Ich.

—Ibsen, as quoted by Thomas Mann

It is hard to realize today that Heinrich Mann (1871–1950) was once considered more important and 'modern' than his younger brother Thomas; that the expressionists revered him as a great forebear and model; that Benn, Brecht, and Rilke praised him eloquently. Doubtless his prestige was exaggerated, but the reaction against it has gone too far. At a minimum, Heinrich Mann will survive for two brilliant satiric novels, *Professor Unrat* and *Der Untertan*, some lucid, moving essays, and the double novel he devoted in exile to Henri IV.* Like some of his novellas, the novel *Die kleine Stadt* has much colour and verve but is not of the first rank.

Owing little to German literature, the older Mann derived largely from Balzac, Flaubert, Zola, and D'Annunzio. (He has been charged with overestimating all things French and Italian; at worst this was a useful counterbalance to the then usual German prejudice.) Fascinated for a period by the Renaissance, he drew heavily on Burckhardt and Nietzsche and the latter's cult of amoral supermen. Yet in politics he was always a man of the liberal left and of reason: the 'hysterical Renaissance' did not beguile him for long, though he characteristically inclined to scepticism about bourgeois morality and to a neo-pagan attitude toward sex. Basically, however, he was a moralist who believed that every intellectual was duty bound to work for the victory of *Geist* over power, internationalism over chauvinism. His development was clearer, more unilinear than his brother's: as a person and a writer, he was far less complex.

Characteristically, Heinrich Mann's first important book was the satire *Im Schlaraffenland* (1900), an extraordinarily biting novel

* For this and his other important writings after 1933, see p. 99.

focused on corruption in Berlin society. The three-volume *Die Göttinnen* recounts the adventures of a sort of superwoman who appears successively in the roles of Diana, Minerva, and Venus. Owing much to D'Annunzio and Nietzsche, the triptych offers orgies as well as *Herrenmoral*; it is painfully dated.

Flöten und Dolche, the title of Mann's next work, reflects the same period; but the most famous of these novellas, 'Pippo Spano,' recalls the more sceptical attitude of his brother Thomas. A neurotic though successful artist tries to emulate the 'Renaissance' behaviour of the *condottiere* Spano. Faced with a scandal, he persuades his mistress to die with him, but after stabbing her, loses his courage and lives on—a 'comedian,' rather like Thomas' Detlev Spinell.* Similarly, *Die kleine Stadt* is a work of transition: a declaration of a sophisticated commitment to democracy. The citizens of the small town, whether liberals or clerical conservatives politically, have a full share of human weakness, as becomes drastically evident when the actresses of a visiting troupe occasion widespread amorous excitement; but they learn to work together effectively (Mann still has some fear that the Italians may yet prove too *mobile*).[1] That the priest performs the most shocking act is credible, from Mann's point of view; but he is allowed, surprisingly, to save his soul by public confession. Mann well knew that it would be extremely difficult to show symbolically the long process of democratizing a nation in an action lasting a few days. By employing an extremely large cast containing no black villains nor shining heroes, he made his point. The composer, modelled on Puccini, is the only genius in the book, and even he has obvious shortcomings.

On the whole, Italy appears as the country of human beings, Germany as that of bullies, clowns, and automata. *Professor Unrat* (1904), the caricature of a pedant, makes this viewpoint evident. *Unrat* is the most mordant of a series of novels protesting against the tyranny and overwork of German schools and *Gymnasia*; Hesse's *Unterm Rad*, Emil Strauss's *Freund Hain*, Musil's more ironic *Die Verwirrungen des Zöglings Törless*, and some late chapters of *Buddenbrooks* are leading examples. Actually, *Unrat* is less protest than satire. The poor pedagogue with his language full of obsolete adverbs ('traun fürwahr!') and clichés seems on balance more an unconscious

* See below, p. 52.

victim of the Prusso-German system than a malicious despot. So at least he appears in the unforgettable film *Der blaue Engel*; but though that is harsh in revealing the fat underbelly of German society, it softens Mann's intention. Emil Jannings' Unrat is pathetic; in the novel, Unrat is motivated by hatred to the end.

Equally harsh is the caricature of the trilogy *Das Kaiserreich*. Only its first part, *Der Untertan* (written 1912–14; not published, significantly, until 1918), is a successful novel. Its hero, Diedrich Hessling, is almost too revolting to be credible. (His first name is extremely 'old German'; his second suggests ugliness as well as hatred.) Not only is he a chauvinist of the worst sort but a complete opportunist: a real pre-Nazi. His Social Democratic antagonist Napoleon [!] Fischer is also corrupt; only the old liberal, a survivor of 1848, is decent, and he is crushed. Mann's parody of *Lohengrin* is very relevant: like Wilhelm II, Hessling sees himself as a knight in shining armour. The second part of the series, *Die Armen*, tells of the sufferings of the proletariat; the third, *Der Kopf*, more or less expressionistic in style, is a *roman à clef* dealing with the ruling clique around the Kaiser.

Mann wrote several dramas of which only *Madame Legros* (1913) is at all memorable. On the whole, it is in his major essays that his most attractive side appears. Such pieces as 'Voltaire-Goethe' and his long 'Zola' (which is thought by some to be the finest essay in German literature) show his admiring empathy for French culture; they have warmth as well as lucidity and eloquence. Thomas Mann once felt that they were uncritically Francophile, the products of a naïve *Zivilisationsliterat*, but later realized that Heinrich had dealt with the world of the present while he himself was still bemused by romantic illusions.

The most renowned of German novelists, and very possibly the greatest, Thomas Mann (1875–1955) also published a long series of novellas, several of them masterpieces, and numerous essays in a literary career of some sixty years. Like the writings of his own Aschenbach, some of his work appealed both to the broad public and to the *avant-garde*, and his *œuvre* is as noteworthy for its sustained quality as for its triumphs; even above this plateau, peaks and one great mountain rise. Unlike Aschenbach, he had an ironic realization of his own failings, humour, and a sense of duty towards others: he developed from a rather snobbish intellectual to 'a good soldier in man's war of liberation.'

Born of a patrician Lübeck family, Thomas Mann long felt guilty for deserting the role of the burgher, but became addicted to writing while still in school. After his father's death, the family moved to Munich; Mann, escaping the Lübeck *Gymnasium* at eighteen, worked and studied briefly there but largely educated himself. Around 1895 he read Nietzsche* and Schopenhauer, whose dogmas that the will is primary and individuation a mere illusion he took very seriously. During a long stay in Italy with Heinrich, Mann began to write *Buddenbrooks*, the stylized presentation of his own family. (His early stories also deal largely with autobiographical motifs and the milieu of Lübeck.) Returning to Munich, he soon became well known; he married in 1905, living thereafter a highly disciplined and—until the rise of Nazism—an outwardly uneventful life.

It was the success of *Buddenbrooks* (1901) which founded his reputation. As so often later, Mann pleased the general taste as well as the particular. On one level, *Buddenbrooks* seems a solid, straightforward family chronicle, rather like the *Forsyte Saga*, with much humour but much dying, solid accounts of solid people but of eccentrics too, poignant conflicts between the individuals' loves and the financial interests of the family. Something for everyone! Yet other aspects of the book are equally important: for Mann this reckoning with his ancestors' world was a liberating step in the long process of 'de-burgherizing' (*Entbürgerlichung*) which he later thought central in his development. In its account of Thomas Buddenbrook's Schopenhauer experience, which could have freed Thomas from taking the business world so seriously, as in its use of the leitmotif for musical effect, the novel is more complex, less old-fashioned, than most readers have realized.

Tristan, a collection of novellas published in 1903, contained the three most brilliant stories Mann had written: 'Gladius Dei'; the title story; and, most famous of all, 'Tonio Kröger.' The first confronts the world of art with a fanatically religious protest against it. Seeing a very sensual Madonna in a Munich art store, a young man, dressed like a monk,[2] protests violently; ejected, he prophesies the

* See above, pp. 21–23.

destruction of the glittering city. Everything is told in a few sharp pages.

'Tristan' unites grotesque comedy with Wagnerian eroticism; as so often, Mann has his cake and eats it. In the Alpine sanatorium 'Einfried' Detlev Spinell, a writer of no importance, falls in love with Gabriele Klöterjahn, whose robust husband has brought her there because of a lung ailment. (As usual in Mann, the proper names are significant: 'Einfried' suggests both 'peace' and 'cemetery,' 'Spinell' is a semi-precious stone, etc.) Although far from prepossessing, Spinell manages to fascinate his 'Isolde'—at which point mordant parody is replaced by eloquent restatement of the myth.

With some reason, readers have complained that the early Mann focused too insistently on a very few themes, above all, on the hostility between burgher and artist (life vs. spirit). In 'Tonio Kröger,' his most lyrical, personal story, he has significantly changed the pattern; his autobiographical hero transcends the old dichotomy; as artist he is attracted by the normality he lacks, affectionately presenting—though with 'the least bit of scorn'—the lives of ordinary people. If, Tonio finally realizes, he wrote without love, with the arrogance of the *fin-de-siècle*, he would sound like a clanging brass. A net of leitmotifs, such as the wild-flower in his father's buttonhole, the old walnut tree, the gypsies in a green wagon, evoke reminiscence and nostalgia much as music does.

Königliche Hoheit (1909) is rare among Mann's early works in its happy ending. Because of its light, fairy-tale-like tone, its direct didacticism and unabashed optimism, German critics have often scorned it; but one doubts that sophisticated readers would take this entertainment as a moral lesson. In its use of imagery, especially of cold colours to symbolize the frigidity of the court, this underrated work shows great artistry.

The most complex of Mann's novellas, *Der Tod in Venedig* (1912) is also the first to make elaborate, consistent use of mythical references. Gradually we become aware that the series of sinister strangers whom the doomed Aschenbach encounters are masks of the same figure—death; and critics[3] have come to see the ambivalence of major figures and motifs: the boy Tadzio represents death as well as Apollonian beauty; the jungle is the home of both death and Dionysiac vitality.—In his stern devotion to his craft, Aschenbach is one of the more virile heroes who replaced the Tonio Krögers and Spinells at the time*—a *Leistungsethiker* who sacrifices everything for the sake of achievement.

Other *Leistungsethiker* of Mann's new phase were Schiller (in the brilliant sketch 'Schwere Stunde') and Frederick II of Prussia. When the war came, amazing Mann, who later admitted how naïve he then was, he made Frederick the hero of the semi-fictional *Friedrich und die grosse Koalition*. While this is not a flag-flapping book, it does show that Mann was seriously infected by the viruses of 1914. The most massive evidence of his infection is his *Betrachtungen eines Unpolitischen* (1918). This long collection of essays is by no means protofascist—towards the end, the author inclines to the democratic side—but it is nationalistic, amateurish, repetitious, and 'unbuttoned.' Yet out of this least of his books grew his greatest—*Der Zauberberg*.†

Mann's near contemporary, Hermann Hesse (1877–1962), is often discussed with him. Profoundly different in style and temperament, the two have much in common: fascination with the 'polarities' of existence, deep concern with the future of Europe and Germany, a tendency to the educational novel (Hesse is even more autobiographical), to *Entbürgerlichung*, to cosmopolitanism. (Hesse rejected nationalism some years before Mann did.)

Perhaps the central factor in Hesse's thought was the inwardness derived from his Swabian pietist background; he secularized it but remained profoundly introverted. Typically, he enthusiastically admired Novalis, with his dictum that 'the way within' leads us to truth. His books abound with transparently veiled 'Hesses': Hermann Lauscher, Harry Haller, H. H., Hermine (his '*anima*'), even Veraguth; or he projects the main aspects of his personality into polar figures like Narziss and Goldmund. His life abounded in crises: at least two near-breakdowns, his rupture with German public opinion in 1914, psychoanalysis, two divorces. (The pietist type may behave no more correctly than others, but feels guilt more sharply.)

Out of these agonies, a major writer finally emerged. As Ziolkowski remarks,[4] Hesse did not achieve a great deal before 1914; but *Der Steppenwolf* is one of the most challenging of novels, *Narziss und Goldmund* and especially *Das Glasperlenspiel* possess serene charm

---

* About another sort of protagonist, Felix Krull, see pp. 98f.
† For this and later works, see below, pp. 94–99.

and wisdom. As *Steppenwolf* proceeds the outsider finally sees that the classicism of Mozart and Goethe is not stodgy; he even accepts, without the scorn of the European 'intellectual,' such American phenomena as jazz, radio, and automobiles. (Even in such early works as *Knulp*, Hesse revealed a saving sense of humour.)

Hesse first became well known as the author of the rather sentimental novel *Peter Camenzind* (1904); two years later his 'school novel' *Unterm Rad* appeared—based on felt experience but not a remarkable work of art. Shortly before the war he wrote *Knulp* (1915), a series of tales about the delightful outcast of that name, which recalls Eichendorff's *Taugenichts* and anticipates Kazantzakis' *Zorba the Greek*. More autobiographical is *Rosshalde*, a novel of domestic tension: the artist Veraguth frees himself painfully from an oppressive, unhappy marriage. These are respectable books but if anything less impressive than those of Ricarda Huch, Wassermann, and other novelists of the second or third magnitude.

After 1914, awakened like Castorp by the 'thunderclap' of war, Hesse became a far more interesting writer. Private and political struggles served as a purgatory. *Demian* (1919) was the first work written by the 'new Hesse.' In some ways, it is embarrassingly adolescent, reflecting the first fine careless rapture of the *Jugendbewegung* on discovering Nietzsche. Yet no one else could have written this intensely alive book; its very vitality may account for its enthusiastic reception.

The protagonist Sinclair, the child of pietist parents, gradually emerges from his stifling cocoon. 'The bird is fighting its way out of the egg' is a major leitmotif. After a particularly unpleasant puberty, he gains a degree of balance, even some glimmerings of maturity, when the outbreak of the First World War brings the book to a sudden close. As in the traditional *Bildungsroman*, Sinclair has a mentor and guide: a somewhat older friend, the sophisticated and precocious Demian. Basically, what Demian teaches Sinclair is to relax a bit his compulsive moralism; but as a work of its time and place, the novel is furnished with a formidable, rather misleading ideology, an amalgam of Christianity, Nietzsche, and Gnosticism.

In his successful efforts to instil some *joie de vivre* into his friend, Demian tells him of the Gnostic god Abraxas, who embraces all of life, not merely good like the Christian God, but also evil. This sounds like *fin-de-siècle* Satanism but is not: poor Sinclair thinks that sex and a normal degree of self-assertion are evil: Demian and 'Abraxas' merely free him from the moralistic obsessions of the pietist and petit bourgeois mind.

At the same time, the theme of polarities overcome in a transcendent unity is central in Hesse. To Hesse and his *personae*, as Ziolkowski well puts it:

> The world . . . just like man . . . is a unity comprising the forces of nature and spirit, night and day, inside and outside, and all other conceivable polar extremes. Ideally these forces are in perfect harmony. . . . Yet more often one pole has ascendancy over the other, and this condition is the basis of all human notions concerning good and evil. . . . Magical thinking is the capacity of the individual to see beyond the apparent disharmony of the polar opposites and to perceive the essential unity and totality of all things. . . .[5]

Unless a man overcomes this bifurcation in his Weltanschauung, he will remain a split personality, indeed a lost soul. Hesse remained basically the religious man in his experience and expression of life, not the least so when he appeared the most heretical.

There has been much speculation about Demian's identity. Is he merely Sinclair himself, cured of neurosis? Or, as the letters of the name suggest, his daimon? The latter seems probable, since another rearrangement would produce 'niema[n]d,' in other words, no one else but the protagonist. In this case, the ambiguity surrounding Sinclair's love for Demian's mother, Frau Eva, dissolves at once. If he and Demian are the same person, it is hardly surprising that he thinks of her as mother as well as beloved. As the name suggests, Eva is in various senses the first woman to Sinclair—a Jungian archetype. Subtlety was not one of Hesse's characteristics.

Like his other interests, Hesse's fascination by India has roots in his own life: his parents had been there for missionary work, and he himself had visited the subcontinent. *Siddhartha* (1922) is the most renowned of several treatments of this milieu; Hesse shifts easily from Christian to Buddhist terms, remaining as religiously oriented as ever. Like *Demian*, this too is a *Bildungsroman*: the young hero seeks fulfilment and inner peace. These he finds only by a process of constant change—of which the river is the great symbol; he must confine himself to neither 'pole' of existence. Thus Siddhartha experiences and then renounces asceticism and love, poverty and luxury, and even the teachings of Buddha himself, in his Nietzschean endeavour to 'become the one he is.'

Besides many novels and shorter narratives, Hesse wrote a number of essays. One collection of these, *Blick ins Chaos*, greatly impressed T. S. Eliot.[6] He was also a talented lyric poet and water-colourist.*

Many novelists, once highly esteemed and widely read, are today forgotten or ignored. In part their political tendency is distasteful, like Hans Grimm's or at the other extreme, J. R. Becher's—and one could instance far crasser examples. Often the shallowness of pseudo-profundity has become evident, as in those muddy puddles, the works of E. G. Kolbenheyer and a mass of others, or the once widely read fiction of Ernst Wiechert. Many once famous books, like the usual *Frauenroman* or the anti-war novel, are too closely tied to a now obsolete issue. In most such cases, though, the fairest verdict would be: good, but not good enough to survive the truly international competition. (The prevalence of translations in Germany is relevant: even second- or third-raters like Thomas Wolfe, Robert Nathan, and Margaret Mitchell promptly appear *auf Deutsch*, along with a mass of novelists from most European languages.) At least two writers deserve rescue (for very different reasons): Ricarda Huch (1864–1947) and Jakob Wassermann (1873–1934).

Highly versatile, Ricarda Huch wrote essays, histories—including two brilliant volumes on German romanticism—and lyrics as well as narratives of various sorts. Everything she wrote is marked by distinction of style; her language often reveals the sensitivity of the poet but is always lucidly structured prose. Her most famous novels are the highly romantic *Erinnerungen von Ludolf Ursleu dem Jüngeren*— old Ursleu recollects the storms of life in the tranquillity of a cloister —and the more realistic *Aus der Triumphgasse*. Her interest in history, always strong, was dominant in her later career. One volume of her *Deutsche Geschichte* was forbidden by the Nazis.

The great forte of Jakob Wassermann was narration: none of his German contemporaries could devise and articulate plots with so much tension, such a wealth of exciting action. Keenly interested in the psychology of persons under great stress, he was often compared

* On Hesse's later books, see pp. 99–101.

with Dostoevsky but lacked true profundity: his least pretentious works are often his best, like the early novel *Die Juden von Zirndorf*. Often his books seem deliberately sensational, yet he was also genuinely concerned with moral matters, as in *Caspar Hauser* with its theme of 'the indolence of the heart,' or the search for justice in *Der Fall Maurizius* (1928). In the Twenties Wassermann was internationally known and often ranked with Thomas Mann. His autobiographical *Mein Weg als Deutscher und Jude* (1921) is moving—and saddening.

5   *Expressionism*

"Die Welt ist da. Es wäre sinnlos, sie zu wiederholen."

—Kasimir Edschmid

Around 1910 yet another 'ism' emerged as a distinct, self-conscious literary school—expressionism or, as it was occasionally called, *Ausdruckskunst*.[1] Again, the term was borrowed from French painting; but this time the Germans were in the van, though of course many of the forerunners of the movement were non-Germans like Strindberg, Dostoevsky, and Whitman, to name only the most important. In fact, Strindberg's later plays, like Wedekind's *Erdgeist*, seem to us today expressionism *avant la lettre*.

Expressionism was a part of the general intellectual and artistic ferment characteristic of the years from about 1890 to 1924. Each year the cultural world seemed to become more varied, exciting, and dissonant. Paris was the capital of that world, but Central Europe was becoming an increasingly important part of it, in happy contrast to its state in the Eighties. In his characteristic ironic vein, Robert Musil described the situation:

. . . suddenly a stimulating fever had arisen. No one really knew what was taking shape; no one could say whether there was to be a new art, a new man, a new morality or perhaps a change in the social structure. Thus everyone made of it whatever suited him. But everywhere people rose up to battle against the old order. Everywhere the man of the hour was suddenly at his post; and— a matter of real importance—men of practical enterprise joined hands with those of intellectual enterprise. Men of talent were developed who would have been suffocated in earlier days or would not have taken any part at all in public life. They were as different as could be, and the contradictions between their goals were unsurpassable. The superman was loved and the subhuman was loved, health and the sun were worshipped and the delicate affection of consumptive girls was worshipped; people enthusiastically professed belief in the hero and belief in the social welfare of everyone; people were devout believers and sceptics, naturalistic and precious; they dreamed of old avenues of trees near castles, autumnal gardens, glassy ponds, hashish, illness, daemonic states —but also of prairies, far-sweeping horizons, of forges and rolling mills, naked fighters, revolts of the enslaved workers, primaeval human couples, and the destruction of society. To be sure, these were contradictory and highly diverse battle cries, but they had a common spirit; if one had dissected that epoch, some such nonsense would have resulted as an angular circle consisting of wooden iron; but in reality everything was blended together into one evanescent glimmering meaning. This illusion, which found its incarnation in the magic date of the century's turning, was so strong that some plunged enthusiastically into the new, still unused century, while others quickly had one last fling in the old one. . . .[2]

Expressionism itself was not a unified movement: there were parties, schisms, international and national orientations, writers committed to political action as well as those of a more mystical, quietist attitude.[3] Yet the term has real meaning: it is not a vague label like 'poetic realism' or 'Biedermeier.' To take an example from the fine arts: an impressionist painting of a horse would differ significantly from a photograph or from a picture by Rosa Bonheur but would still be basically a re-presentation; whereas if an expressionist painter, in this case Franz Marc, wished to 'ex-press' a certain emotion evoked in him by horses, he would and did make the animals red or blue.

Two passages may illustrate the general tone of these writers. Thus to paraphrase Kasimir Edschmid, at the time a fervent adherent of the new school:

> We expressionists do not work as photographers but are overcome by visions. We do not try to catch the momentary effect of a situation but its eternal significance; are concerned not with descriptions but lived experience. We do not reproduce but create, . . . in an atmosphere of continual excitement.[4]

And Kurt Pinthus declared, in his introduction to the major anthology of expressionist verse, *Menschheitsdämmerung*:

> Never was . . . the principle of *l'art pour l'art* so flouted as in this poetry, which we call . . . expressionism because it is all eruption, explosion, intensity—must be, to break through every hostile crust. Therefore it avoids naturalistic description of reality . . .; rather, it produces its means of expression, with mighty, violent energy from the . . . power of the spirit itself. . . . Thus social conditions are not presented in realistic detail, as a portrayal of misery . . . but are always transformed into the universal, the great ideas of mankind. And even the war is not shown with objective realism—it is always shown as a vision (indeed, long before it broke out). . . .
>
> Never in world literature did the shriek, the fall, the longing of an age ring out so loudly, laceratingly, and startlingly. . . .[5]

Extending from the very early years of the new century until about 1924, expressionism reached its height around 1917–20, when increasing misery led to bolder protest. In 'late' expressionism, disillusion with the peace of Versailles and the Weimar Republic gradually eroded the original enthusiasm; Brecht's early dramas are cases in point. With the apparent stabilization of German society a few years later, the 'cool,' conversational tone of 'new objectivity' (*Neue Sachlichkeit*) replaced the expressionist scream of ecstasy or horror. In any case, few men can remain in a state of storm and stress indefinitely.

Expressionism characteristically asserts the primacy of the inner world. Its poets make statements about types and pure essences; 'the son,' 'the father,' 'the poet' figure in their dramas. Thus there is no more interest in the psychology of the individual than in naturalistic detail; mimesis is totally rejected.

Many expressionists call for 'the new man'; hence *Wandlung* (transformation) is a key term. In some undefinable way the 'new man' was to combine the best features of Jesus, Faust, and Nietzsche's Zarathustra. The socially 'committed' activists in the movement called for a new society as well. Typically, their political attitude was leftist and pacifistic but not Marxist; materialism was anathema to most of them. Rather, a poet like Werfel will declare that all

mankind is his brother, hailing man as 'O Mensch!' And the minor
dramatist Paul Kornfeld asserts:

> Jeder Mensch ist auserwählt—

a cheerful if somewhat beery sentiment. Such writers protest too
much, and one recalls the statement of Lessing's Francisca: 'One
seldom talks about the virtue one really has.'[6]

To turn back to the forerunners of expressionism: the most important were Dostoevsky and August Strindberg. Dostoevsky's
religiosity appealed, like Strindberg's: his radical morality and intensity made him seem an expressionist himself. In the native tradition too the most intense writers were the most highly valued:
J. M. R. Lenz, Kleist, and Büchner. Walt Whitman's free form and
gospel of democratic love were influential, as were the ethics of the
old Tolstoy.

Even in his so-called naturalistic dramas of the Eighties, like *The
Father* and *Miss Julie*, Strindberg revealed an intensity in action and
imagery which is anything but realistic: fortunately, one does not
often encounter Strindbergian types. But it is to the later Strindberg
that expressionism is mainly indebted—to dramas like *A Dream Play*
and *To Damascus*. (Over a thousand performances of his plays were
staged in Germany in the years 1913–15.)[7] Here the young Germans
found the break with conventional dramatic form, the use of typical
figures and long monologues. From him they took the 'I-drama,'
focused like the *Bildungsroman* on a single evolving personality;
and the 'station drama,' showing, in an analogy to the stations of the
Cross, the stages and ordeals a man must go through. Obviously, the
two often coincide. His portrayal of 'limit situations'—agonies and
ecstasies, especially extremes of suffering—was widely imitated.

The impact of Frank Wedekind's dramas reinforced that of
Strindberg's. As his name implies, Benjamin Franklin Wedekind
(1864–1918) was a libertarian, a cosmopolitan, and from a conventionally German point of view, an outsider. (His father, disillusioned
by the failure of the revolutions of 1848, left Germany for North
America, returning sixteen years later.) In the Eighties, Frank
Wedekind plunged into the colourful life of Munich: besides writing
plays and prose, he acted, sang his own ballads in the cabaret 'Eleven
Executioners,' worked for the satirical journal *Simplizissimus*—he

once spent six months in jail for *lèse-majesté*. Superficially he was a gay fellow with a flair for parody and 'gallows humour' and a consuming hatred of *Kitsch*. Many thought him a clown; he wished to be regarded a tragedian and a thinker. There is two-edged irony here: Wedekind was no clown, but no philosopher either. While he was much aware of the tragic side of life, he is at his best in the high-spirited verve of *Erdgeist*, the caricatures in *Frühlings Erwachen*, and the madcap, often 'black' humour of his dialogue and action.

As a dramatist Wedekind was most indebted to Büchner and Strindberg, as a thinker to Nietzsche. The swift succession of short scenes in *Frühlings Erwachen* recalls *Woyzeck*, as does the mingling of naturalistic and grotesque touches. Wedekind found a similar combination of the realistic and the expressionistic in plays like *Miss Julie*. He also shared the gloomy Swede's obsession with sex and the *femme fatale*, but his tone is radically different: he thought the battle of the sexes a Good Thing. In fact, he carried out Nietzsche's precept to 'live dangerously.' Although physically misshapen, he was, to use his own terms, a *Hopp-hopp Mensch* who lived zestfully, not one of the 'etepetete'—the finicky and overcautious. To him the cardinal factors of life were power and sex: only the strong can be free. Thus he was, unapologetically, a 'tough' Nietzschean.[7] Some have thought him a Satanist, but surely that is to take his more cynical epigrams, and other efforts to shock the Philistines, too seriously. Imbued with ardent hatred of hypocrisy, and convinced that man could be reformed by sexual emancipation and other breaches of convention, he was a sincere if simplistic moralist.[8]

Frühlings Erwachen (1891) was Wedekind's first impressive work. Rather surprisingly, it remains one, though the theme—adolescents should learn the 'facts of life'—could hardly be more dated, nor could the mother ashamed to enlighten her daughter seem more incredible. When catastrophe strikes, two of these blindfolded children die, one as a suicide, another because of an abortion insisted on by her parents; the pathos is real. Even worse than the parents are the schoolmasters, savagely presented in their cowardly stupidity and bearing such names as Kahlbauch, Sonnenstich, and Zungenschlag. Of course this is caricature, but if contemporary society was half as stuffy as this, it was not Satanic to satirize it. At the end of the drama, all realism is abandoned: when the youth whose girl has died walks through the cemetery, he meets his friend, the suicide, with his head under his arm. A masked man, probably Wedekind[9] himself, prevents a second suicide, restoring the boy's courage to live.

Erdgeist (1895), with its somewhat less brilliant sequel *Die Büchse der Pandora*, is the most energetic and exciting of Wedekind's plays; it is perhaps the first truly expressionist play in German literature. The almost irresistible Lulu, a woman beyond good and evil, dispatches one lover after another; despite this super-Strindbergian slaughter, it is a high-spirited work, partly because of amusingly 'off-beat' dialogue, partly since, whatever Wedekind's intentions, one cannot take things too seriously: how frequent or typical is Lulu, after all? Further, the 'bedroom-farce' technique, with lovers hiding everywhere, hardly puts one in a tragic mood. The prologue introduces her, in the guise of a snake, with great gusto. We are in a circus: the animal tamer boasts—after transparent sarcasms directed at Hauptmann's weak heroes—

> Das *wahre* Tier, das *wilde, schöne* Tier
> Das—meine Damen!—sehn Sie nur bei mir . . . !

Lulu is indeed wild, beautiful, and animal, completely ruthless but basically innocent. Gradually it becomes evident that she represents the 'eternal feminine'—*pace* Goethe—she is an archetype: no one knows her age or her father. Yet she is an individual, with her own peculiar wit. All men, idealizing her, see her and name her differently: Eva, Mignon, etc. Since a strong man can master her, she cannot be thought immoral, in Wedekindian terms. Yet in *Die Büchse der Pandora*, where she sinks into degradation and is slain by Jack the Ripper, Wedekind seems to admit that her paths, however exhilarating, lead but to the grave. Similarly, in *Franziska* (1911), the heroine settles down cheerfully with her child after a long series of Faustian adventures. Wedekind was softening—or maturing.

Much of Wedekind's attractiveness is due to his wit, which in turn largely resides in his style. Often the characteristic modern failure to communicate is emphasized: a burgher, interrogating the author of a ballet, confuses its subject, the Dalai Lama, with Nietzsche. There are Wildean bits, like: 'Sin is a mythological name for deals which don't work out.' More characteristic is the remark of the swindler Marquis von Keith, in the drama of that name, when driven out of Munich by 'respectable' people far sharper than he: 'Life is a toboggan slide.' This Keith appears as the great anti-moralist, with a flair for cynicism. Love of God, he holds, is only a symbol of self-love. Yet he has a certain generosity: believing in the values of this world, he tries to make a wretched melancholiac capable of enjoyment.

König Nicolo oder So ist das Leben (1901), a very autobiographical tragedy, is perhaps Wedekind's most serious work. Driven from his throne by a revolution of the philistines, Nicolo-Wedekind becomes a famous actor but is confined to comic roles; when he writes tragedies people think them parodies. Finally, after Nicolo has died as court fool, the new king (an ex-butcher) has him buried in the royal crypt. *Ride, Pagliacci!*

Along with various essays and some less successful plays, Wedekind wrote a number of novellas. One of them, 'Der Brand von Egliswyl,' has been compared with Kleist. In his subject matter, he is hardly an expressionist, but he equalled, and often surpassed, most of that group in his mastery of the grotesque, his bold portrayal of extreme characters—archetypes or caricatures—and his effective distortion of language. For writers of his type, W. H. Sokel has pointed out, 'distortion reveals essence.'[10]

As the primary literary interest of expressionism lies not in its attitudes but in its handling of the language, it seems sensible first to treat the lyric, in which, even more than elsewhere, 'every word counts.' The most important poets were Ernst Stadler, Franz Werfel, Gottfried Benn* (the prime example of the 'ice-cold' attitude assumed by a minority of the group), Georg Heym, Else Lasker-Schüler, August Stramm, and Georg Trakl. There were many others. Consisting mainly of young men, the movement suffered particularly heavy losses during the war.

Some of these writers, like Werfel and Stadler, are expressionistic in theme and attitude but largely traditional in form. The radicals, however, distorted the language boldly, aiming at a maximum of dynamism. Accordingly, they expanded the role of the verb: often verbs are massed together, adjectives or nouns are transformed to verbs—thus *monden, nackten*—or adjectives expressing action are

* Since Benn did not become famous until a much later date, his poems are treated below, pp. 130–133.

coined from verbs: thus 'die schlafe Erde,' 'den keuchen Tod.' In general, these poets do not describe: nature tends to appear only as a symbol of the soul. Articles, being weak little words, are largely pushed out; violent words, often verbal compounds, abound. Traditional punctuation largely vanishes, though exclamation points are unsurprisingly rife. Complex sentences, being too 'intellectual,' are rare: the expressionist lyric tends to very short phrases but also to long lines à la Whitman. In Stramm, the most extreme of all, grammar barely survives. He writes, at the end of 'Abendgang':

> Die Pappel hängt herauf
> Und
> Hebt die Erde nach
> Die schlafe Erde armt den nackten Himmel
> Du schaust und schauerst
> Deine Lippen dünsten
> Der Himmel küsst
> Und
> Uns gebärt der Kuss!

The point of view is that of a woman lying on her back—thus 'the poplar hangs upward'—and the distortion of language contributes to the vertiginous effect.

Often the expressionists aimed at unexpected, drastic, and shocking effects. Benn writes of a cancer ward and of a 'little aster' which falls into a cadaver, Trakl is fascinated by putrefaction, Heym's 'Ophelia' begins 'Im Haar ein Nest von jungen Wasserratten.' In other moods the imagery may evoke the power of machines and factories or suggest celestial bliss: extremes prevail. Of course poets with a religious or political mission, such as Werfel often propounded, must state it understandably, even at the sacrifice of originality.

Actually the themes of very many expressionistic poems are such that a didactic tone is appropriate. In *Menschheitsdämmerung* the verses are grouped under four main headings: 'Sturz und Schrei,' 'Erweckung des Herzens,' 'Aufruf und Empörung,' and 'Liebe den Menschen': at least three of these imply a 'message.' Social subjects are frequent, as in naturalism; but now the aim is the scream (the famous *Schrei*) or shout, not close observation. Brotherhood is the key virtue: one should cherish fraternal feelings toward all humans, and even to animals or trees. Thus Werfel, for example, can regress rapidly from the sublime to the ridiculous. The early expressionists believed that while men are good as such, 'the masses' are particularly virtuous. Thus when disillusion came, in the early Twenties, it was especially bitter.

Believing that the ultimate reality is metaphysical, the expressionists were often religiously oriented. 'Neu Geschlecht dringt hin zu Gott,' as Reinhard Johannes Sorge put it. Unfortunately they often struck a pose of martyrdom.[11] Also, as in Dostoevsky, the diabolical is a close neighbour of the angelic. A strange ambiguity is typical of many of these writers. When love does not appear transcendently beautiful, it is sheer animality; the poet entranced by Christ can revel in decay. In expressionistic dramas, the protagonist who has been presented as a noble God-seeker may gratuitously commit cruel and revolting acts.

The most difficult of the major expressionistic lyricists and, with Benn, the subtlest and most challenging, was Georg Trakl (1887–1914). Like many of his generation he died early in the war; after seeing the horrors of the battle of Grodek, he took an overdose of narcotics. Oppressed by guilt feelings because of a violent passion for his sister, he had become addicted to drugs and alcohol. Yet this Austrian Rimbaud produced, in his two volumes, an *œuvre* which many rank with Rilke's. The major influences on Trakl's poetry would seem to include Hölderlin, Rilke, Baudelaire, Rimbaud, Dostoevsky, and perhaps Nietzsche and Hofmannsthal, but essentially he is as original as any poet born into a tradition can be.

Except in his most Hölderlinian poems, Trakl is closer to the French lyric tradition than to the German. It is not easy to grasp the import of his symbols or know to what realms his metaphors relate; critics tend to speak of 'ciphers' in his poetry. Always, though, a mood is established, always a sense of beauty, though that may be inextricably entwined with ugliness or the sense of doom or both. Martin Heidegger has shown that Trakl's use of various colours—colour is of central importance in his poetry—has constant and yet ambivalent significance: thus 'green' implies decay *and* bloom, 'white' is pale and pure, 'silver' denotes death and the stars.[12]

This accords with Trakl's frequent juxtaposition of extreme

beauty with crass ugliness. (Of course this is typically expressionistic, but here extraordinary poetry is produced.) Thus, to take one example of many:

> Wieder nachtet die Stirne in mondenem Gestein;
> Ein strahlender Jüngling
> Erscheint die Schwester in Herbst und schwarzer Verwesung.

No one can present more gloomy images; the first two lines of 'De Profundis' run:

> Es ist ein Stoppelfeld, in das ein schwarzer Regen fällt.
> Es ist ein brauner Baum, der einsam dasteht.—

yet the last are:

> Im Haselgebüsch
> Klangen wieder kristallne Engel.

Some of his less dark poems are devoted to the youth Elis. Some lines seem to suggest that he possesses godlike qualities:

> Ein Dornenbusch tönt,
> Wo deine mondenen Augen sind.
> O, wie lange bist, Elis, du verstorben.

In its solemnity, deliberate movement, and simple monumentality of statement, Trakl's verse is close to Hölderlin's. These hardly expressionistic traits should remind us that a true writer cannot be fitted into any pigeon-hole. The line 'Die Stufen des Wahnsinns in schwarzen Zimmern' recalls his great predecessor in a more melancholy way.

Possibly the most striking note in Trakl's poetry is the sense of doom—'Hirten begruben die Sonne im kahlen Wald.' With him it was all too genuine, too well founded; unlike so many, he did not exploit his sufferings, he expressed them.

To turn to a very different type of literature, the Dadaist movement arose as protest against expressionism, which it thought decadent; yet in a larger context, it reveals close ties to the more experimental expressionistic poets, such as August Stramm. In the spring of 1916 a group of extremely *avant-garde*, radically pacifistic writers joined to found the Cabaret Voltaire in Zurich. Two of its members, Hans Arp (1887–1966) and Hugo Ball (1886–1927) came across the word Dada in a French dictionary. To quote a third founder, Richard Huelsenbeck:

> Dada wurde in einem Lexikon gefunden, es bedeutet nichts.
> Dies ist das bedeutende Nichts, an dem nichts etwas bedeutet.[13]

In a less epigrammatic vein, Huelsenbeck wrote that Dada signified 'abstract art, broadly speaking.'[14]

Convinced that the contemporary world was a madhouse, the Dadaists aimed to convey a sense of the paradoxical, grotesque, and absurd. Unlike most of the expressionists, the Dadaists have a marked comic strain, especially evident in the poems of Arp: *Der vogel selbdritt* and *Die wolkenpumpe* (both 1920) are characteristically entitled collections of his verse.

Aside from painting, Dada made its main contribution in the lyric, and Arp was the foremost German poet of the group. In his milder works, he carried on the tradition of Morgenstern; he too was fascinated by the sight and sound of words as such; thus he wrote in 'sankt ziegenzack':

> sankt ziegenzack springt aus dem ei
> rumsdiebums das gigerltum
> vergissmeinnicht rollt um den stuhl
> glocke schlägt nur eins und zwei

In a manifesto of 1918, various Dadaists listed the simultaneous, the 'bruitistic [noisy],' and the static poem as new genres. The first type aims to present the confusing mass of impressions which strike the psyche in a great city:

> Das SIMULTANISTISCHE GEDICHT lehrt den Sinn des
> Durcheinanderjagens aller Dinge, während Herr Schulze
> liest, fährt der Balkanzug über die Brücke bei Nisch,
> ein Schwein jammert im Keller des Schlächters Nuttke.

Often the Dadaists emancipated themselves completely from meaning to produce pure visual and auditory patterns, as in Hugo Ball's 'Katzen und Pfauen':

baubo sbugl ninga gloffa

siwi faffa
sbugi faffa
olofa fafamo
faufo halja finj

Basically an international movement—two of its founders were Rumanians—Dada soon shifted from Zurich to great centres like Paris and Berlin. Indeed, Hugo Ball himself came to feel, a few months after the movement had been launched, that it had no more to say;[15] and actually it had a tendency to degenerate into a mere fad. As a European phenomenon, however, it influenced surrealistic poetry, painting, and cinema; and such contemporary German poets as Helmut Heissenbüttel are indebted to it.

In the drama as in the lyric, a number of talented writers appeared: Carl Sternheim, Georg Kaiser, Ernst Barlach, Fritz von Unruh, Franz Werfel, and later Ernst Toller and Bertolt Brecht, as well as such lesser figures as Sorge, Walter Hasenclever, Paul Kornfeld, and Oskar Kokoschka (whose main gift was for painting). There was no single dominant dramatist; Brecht did not become a major writer until long after the expressionistic storm had subsided.

Even more than in the days of naturalism, the stage functioned as a pulpit, and the 'sermons' treated a great variety of private and public problems. As a kind of youth movement which arrayed the 'sons' against the 'fathers'—a favourite theme of the expressionists' dramas—they were especially impressed by Nietzsche's demand 'Break the old tablets'; like him, they felt that man should be an 'arrow of longing for the other shore.' Like Strindberg in *To Damascus*, the expressionists used the 'station drama' to write about their own lives. Sternheim and Kaiser satirized the middle class; Kaiser, Unruh, and others celebrated the hoped-for 'new man,' higher and nobler than the men of today. Toller, who had himself been transformed from an enthusiastic soldier to a pacifist, wrote of *Wandlung*, and exposed the evils of capitalism, as did Kaiser and others. Increasingly, as the war went on, writers denounced it in plays not stageable before 1918; Kaiser warned of an even greater catastrophe to come. As the crisis deepened, social and political revolution became a more significant theme than the revolt against one's parents. Soon after 1919, the leading dramatists lost their optimistic faith in social action: the new man failed to appear, the new society was a disappointment. Toller no longer could believe in the masses; Kaiser's *Gas II* ends with the annihilation of the world; Unruh could not finish the trilogy intended to hail the advent of a better age.

From almost any aspect, the expressionistic drama is marked by extremes and violent contrasts. It is largely peopled by typical, and at times archetypal characters, especially 'the son,' 'the daughter,' 'the father,' yet often, notably in Kaiser's plays, the persons are barely more than automata: 'man in yellow,' 'third man in grey,' 'fourth worker,' etc. Like Kaiser in *Die Koralle*, Franz Werfel uses the *Doppelgänger* (double) in his *Spiegelmensch*, a technique appropriate to 'split,' two-souled protagonists. Although these writers tend to follow the gallant masculine tradition that the female sex is the nobler, women in their plays often appear obsessed with incestuous or nymphomaniac desire or as hopelessly dull middle-class housewives.

Often expressionistic acting and staging proved far more effective than the plays themselves.[16] From 1918 to 1933 the Berlin theatre was as interesting as any in existence. (Even the Nazis did not completely ruin it.) Great directors like Max Reinhardt and Leopold Jessner had a cadre of highly competent actors at their disposal—as well as unlimited modern gadgets like filmstrips, loudspeakers, 'spots' and other sources of light. Generally the stage was very sparsely furnished. As naturalism was *passé*, the audience was expected to use its imagination. Backdrops, like those of Georg Grosz, tended towards caricature and a rather heavy-handed symbolism. Frequently the stage had several physical levels: scenes could be shown simultaneously.[17] At the end of Kaiser's *Die Bürger von Calais*, the lower stage shows the end of the hero's life literally, while the upper scene is symbolic. Great crowds (of workers or soldiers, typically) often appeared on stage; authors aimed at choral effects.

In its themes, the expressionist drama contained both soaring idealism and utter sordidness, often in the same play. Thus Unruh's *Ein Geschlecht*, a powerful denunciation of war, urges 'a new, human ethic' but is itself largely concerned with incest and rape; Werfel's

Bocksgesang, like his *Spiegelmensch,* is marked by harsh dissonances. Nothing is considered too ugly or grotesque for the stage. The protagonist of Toller's *Hinkemann,* emasculated by a wound incurred in the war, makes his living by biting through the throats of rats and mice at public fairs. While most of the expressionists did no doubt believe in peace, beauty, and goodness, many were at least equally devoted to the old bohemian aim of shocking the bourgeoisie. Yet the intention is generally didactic: there is endless rhetoric about peace, revolution, the new man, and so on. Musil showed his usual acuity in naming the expressionistic poet in *Der Mann ohne Eigenschaften* 'Feuermaul.'

Carl Sternheim, however, the first dramatically gifted writer of the group to emerge, was cool to the point of coldness and ironic if not cynical about human motivation. A bit older than the other playwrights—he lived from 1878 to 1942—Sternheim has much in common with Wedekind; his satire is even more biting. With a sure sense of comic and of theatrical effect, Sternheim presents a harsh, disillusioned society. His characters are curiously two-dimensional, having passions and ambition but lacking emotion. This of course frustrated his hope of becoming the German Molière.

Yet in a series of comedies published together as *Aus dem bürgerlichen Heldenleben* (1922), Sternheim showed insight into the sordid side of German life as well as wit. The family figuring most prominently in this sequence is significantly named Maske; we are gradually led to the conclusion that they, and the burghers generally, are no worse than the other classes; they are ruthless social climbers but determined and down to earth.

The most famous of these plays, *Die Hose* (1911) takes its name from the underpants which the attractive Frau Luise Maske loses in public. (Questions of taste did not greatly bother the expressionists.) Attracted by this event, both a self-styled Nietzschean intellectual and a neurasthenic Wagnerite barber rent rooms at the Maskes', which leads to ludicrous situations but to no affair. At the end, having improved his financial situation—and incidentally seduced his wife's confidante—Maske tells Luise that they can now afford a child.

Their offspring appears in the appropriately named *Der Snob.* After paying off his mistress and his parents, who obligingly move

away, young Maske marries into the aristocracy and then, discovering that simple parents are now chic, recalls them.

Thus in theme Sternheim is hardly expressionistic; it is the distorted language his characters use which allies him to the movement. For example, one asserts: 'Es liebt sie—Du?' and another
bitterly notes: 'Ja Prolet [bin ich] missduftend.' While he published
narrative fiction* and an autobiography, Sternheim is memorable
mainly as a dramatist. His anti-romantic stance allies this 'ice-
cooled expressionist' to Brecht and Benn.

Sternheim's skilful dramatic structure links him to a more productive, once world-famous writer, Georg Kaiser (1878–1945). Someone has noted that his expressionistic plays were the first German
products accepted by the West after 1918.† Kaiser's very keen
'dialectic' mind recalls Hegel; his careful working out of problems
often reduces his characters to chessmen but can be fascinating. The
most ingenious writer on German expressionistic drama, Bernhard
Diebold, described Kaiser as the *Denkspieler* of the theatre, which is
in line with the playwright's own remark that the greatest dramatist
was—Plato.

In the uneven mass of Kaiser's production, several dramas stand out
clearly; two or three have moments of greatness. After publishing
several lesser plays, notably comedies dealing with sex, he wrote the
intensely expressionistic *Von Morgens bis Mitternachts* in 1912 (pub.
1916). The action of this 'station drama' moves with frantic speed.
Tired of his life of quiet desperation, a bank clerk embezzles a large
sum and rushes out into the world in the hope of gaining life in
return for money. This petit bourgeois Faust encounters one dis-
illusioning shock after another; he learns the hard way that what is
buyable is not worth having. Appropriately, the climax comes in a
great hall during a six-day bicycle race, a symbol of the rat race of
life. In a moment of insight, the clerk confesses and repents his guilt.
Betrayed by a Salvation Army girl anxious to claim the reward for
his arrest—the ironic twist is typical of Kaiser—he commits suicide.
At the end Kaiser compares this poor nameless wretch to Christ—
a lamentable lapse.

* See below, pp. 80f.

† Kaiser tried his hand at a number of styles and types of drama, but figures
in this book only as an expressionist; I shall discuss only a handful of the some
sixty plays he wrote.

There are many striking touches: thus when the clerk takes shelter under a tree, the audience sees Death in the branches above him. The bicycle race scene is arch-expressionistic in its wildly excited crowd and spectacular lighting effects. When the clerk leaves home before dinner, this breach of the family's 'sacred' habits actually kills his mother. *Von Morgens bis Mitternachts* is satiric allegory: the clerk is an Everyman lost in a chaotic society which offers only the choice between the dullest routine or crime.

Written as a warning against war in 1913, *Die Bürger von Calais* was staged four years later, when hope for peace was becoming quite respectable; it made Kaiser famous.[18] His immediate inspiration was Rodin's group statue, based on Froissart's chronicle, of the six burghers willing to sacrifice themselves to save their city from destruction by the English king, who finally pardons them.

The application to Kaiser's own time was clear: the sacrificial burghers had to oppose their new morality to the deluded courage of the war party, determined to fight to the last man. Eustache de Saint-Pierre, a 'new man' in the expressionistic sense, convinces the majority that the true, humble, deed—preserving the city—outweighs all heroics.

Kaiser's most important innovation was to involve seven citizens in the threat of death, although the king demanded only six hostages. Any one of them could easily save himself, but Eustache commits suicide to save the others from this temptation. As often, Kaiser's love of dialectics leads him to far-fetched notions, but this remains one of his best plays. In his sacrificial death, Eustache is a more convincing Christ figure than the bank clerk.

In line with the expressionistic faith in man, Kaiser pointed the way to a better society in *Hölle Weg Erde*, but his darkly pessimistic *Gas* trilogy (1917–20) is far more characteristic. (The first play, *Die Koralle*, is mainly interesting as background.) Gas is a multivalent symbol: it refers to capitalism but above all to the dangerously dynamic drives in man and society which lead to conflict. Compulsively, the engineer, the business men, and not least the workers labour at producing the lethal stuff; essentially, they work not for money or self-aggrandizement but because it is their job. (As in Kafka's *Der Prozess*, the cult of work for its own sake, regardless of its intrinsic values, is brilliantly exposed.) Although the engineer's figures were 'correct,' the factory explodes: the best calculations cannot cope with the crisis. Only one man, the son of the billionaire of *Die Koralle*, opposes the suicidal system. The workers refuse his primitivistic, 'back to nature' solution; finally he yields to the pressure of the government, business men, and the workers themselves; the factory will be rebuilt. Now he no longer believes in innate human goodness, and when his sister proclaims that she will give birth to the 'new man,' one wonders.

Gas II carries the allegory to the ultimate. After a lost war the Chief Engineer, to sabotage the plans of the occupiers, persuades the workers to manufacture poison gas, despite the admonition of the 'new man' that 'the kingdom is not of this world.' Defeated, he sets off the explosion: the trilogy ends in complete mutual destruction. The Day of Judgment has come. Remarkably enough, Kaiser predicted not only the war and the defeat and ensuing intransigence of Germany, but the invention of an absolute weapon.

In terms of stage effect, these two plays are Kaiser's great accomplishment. Colour symbolism is central: the gas turns red as the explosion nears, a man in white (Death?) warns of the impending catastrophe, etc. Great mass scenes take place in the colossal factory. Cast in Kaiser's 'telegram style,' the grotesque language is starkly effective: thus the Chief Engineer expresses his hatred for the victors, in *Gas II*: 'Absinkt Hand und ballt Faust gegen euch— abschwingt Fuss und nimmt Anlauf gegen euch. . . .' The frenzied workers shout, as they seem to think, in slogans: 'Gas! ! ! !' later gives way to 'Giftgas! ! !'

The expressionistic plays of Fritz von Unruh (b. 1885) treat the same period with equal intensity, but he is generally warmer, more emotional than Kaiser. His early dramas, notably *Louis Ferdinand, Prinz von Preussen*, centre on the theme of military obedience and owe much to Kleist. A cavalry officer, he denounced militarism by the fall of 1914;[19] his *Ein Geschlecht* (pub. 1918) is perhaps the most powerful of the many anti-war plays.

The word *Geschlecht* denotes here a family, a generation, and the human race; so it is appropriate that the family whose struggles and sufferings are presented is an archetypal one. Unable to adjust themselves to the savagery of war, one of the three sons has committed rape, another shown himself a coward; both are to be executed; the daughter refuses to bear children in a warlike world. Although the mother's earlier support of war has incurred her children's hatred, she atones by snatching from the officer his staff, symbolic of militarism and masculinity in general, and by her (voluntary) death. The father does not appear, but it is significant that the concept of a father god is rejected. Hope lies in the Youngest Son, who leads his comrades, at the end of the play, to storm the 'barracks of violence.'

Written only a few years later, *Platz* (1920) reflects the disillusion which set in after 1918. It continues the account of the surviving members of the symbolic family. Dietrich, the Youngest Son, vainly endeavours to found a new society, based on love, but finds such an ideal realizable only in his personal life. The third part of the trilogy, 'Dietrich,' written in exile, is still unpublished. Both plays are written in verse, with much use of symbols, like the staff or the fire lily, emblem of love and life, in *Platz*. The language, like the action, tends towards violence and hectic eroticism.

Obscured during the heyday of expressionism, Ernst Barlach (1870-1938) obtained recognition rather late; today he appears as one of its authentic talents, not least because he followed no party line. Unlike most writers of the movement, he distrusted abstractions not rooted in earthy reality, and in one of his strongest dramas, *Der tote Tag* (1912), he upheld the 'father principle'—light, spirit, and life—against the 'chthonic' forces symbolized in the mother. Such opposition to the stylish mode of symbolic patricide is typical of Barlach's independence.

Possibly Barlach's statues and etchings are more distinguished than his written works, but both are important and both make the same statement. In his most characteristic works one has a tragic sense of the crushing weight of life, and of *Angst*. Truly a 'Gothic man,' Barlach develops the grotesque and bizarre as a counterbalance to tragedy—but these are only gargoyles on the cathedral. Barlach was deeply moved by travelling in Russia in 1906; his dramas are full of Dostoevskian and Tolstoian touches—the frenzied religiosity of the one, the humaneness of the other. Like Rilke and several lesser writers, he shared the delusion—in some cases a productive one—that the 'Russian soul' is somehow more Christlike than any other. Whatever the influences on him, his plays like his sculptures are marked by humanity and genuine concern with religious values.

Only those who sense that there is 'something beyond,' as does Fräulein Isenbarn in *Der arme Vetter*, can be saved. By no means orthodox, Barlach championed 'the developing (*werdenden*) God' against the traditional concept.

Der tote Tag is characteristic of Barlach in its strength, sincerity, and its perhaps involuntary grotesqueness. He has located his myth in the grey world of a joyless northern heathenism. The son tries to free himself from his mother; his father (God, the spirit) has sent a magic horse to aid him. When the son loses his struggle against a symbolic nightmare, his selfish, possessive mother kills the steed and prevails over him. He reverts to childhood; eventually both he and his wrongly victorious mother commit suicide. 'Strange, that man cannot learn that his father is God,' as one character puts it. Three Wagnerian dwarves, the gargoyles of the piece, largely set its tone.

Der arme Vetter (1918) is Barlach's most poignant work: it presents various persons spending Easter holidays at a resort near Hamburg, and its basic theme is, appropriately, resurrection. In essence we have a triangle—the outsider, Hans Iver, who has tried to kill himself but is a true *Mensch*; his opposite, the appropriately named Siebenmark; and Siebenmark's fiancée Fräulein Isenbarn. Needless to say, she comes to prefer Hans Iver. Barlach has embedded his symbolic action in a mass of realistic, grotesque detail.

It is typical of Barlach that Fräulein Isenbarn—the real hero of the play?—undergoes a radical transformation (*Wandlung*). Similarly, Boll, the protagonist of *Der blau Boll*, judges himself, dies, and is reborn. No modern writer has presented a 'Gothic' philosophy more sincerely than Barlach. His limitation, in literature and the fine arts, is simply the other side of the coin: one scans his works in vain for classic joy or beauty.

Radically different from Barlach's as it is, the work of Ernst Toller (1893–1939) is marked by a similar honesty; his life testifies to his integrity and humaneness. The child of well-to-do Jewish parents, Toller volunteered for front service in 1914, partly in the hope that this would gain him acceptance despite his 'race.' The horrors of the war soon changed his entire view of life. Invalided from the army, he returned to Germany; he became a militant socialist and an outspoken pacifist. The authorities condemned him to some months' imprisonment. In 1919 he became one of the chiefs of the bizarre

Soviet 'republic' in Munich; he did his best to restrain it from un-necessary bloodshed. After its collapse he was sentenced to five years in prison (see his volume of poems *Das Schwalbenbuch* and his auto-biographical *Eine Jugend in Deutschland* about his existence there). His plays reflect his successive disillusionments: with Germany, the social revolution, and 'the masses,' but he never became cynical; even his satiric *No More Peace* (1937) is more amusing than bitter. He left Germany in 1932. Like many other victims of Nazism, he perished in exile; he committed suicide in 1939. Presumably he found the prospect of another war too much to bear.

Die Wandlung (1919), a 'station drama,' is symbolic autobio-graphy. Friedrich,* the protagonist, is transformed from an ardent nationalist to a 'new man.' Having sensed the rottenness of the social structure, he is 'reborn' and can persuade the people to a spiritual as well as practical revolution. Significantly, the author states on the first page: 'The action plays in Europe before the renascence (*Wiedergeburt*).' Realistic scenes alternate with dream-pictures which point out, often grotesquely, the meaning of events; most ghostly is a weird dance of skeletons.

In *Masse Mensch*, published the following year, disillusion has already set in. Not that Toller reverted to the conservative side, then or later, but he now realized that the masses, as an ideal, are 'Moloch,' like God or the state. In fact, any materialism is 'Moloch': Toller did not long remain an orthodox Marxist. A revolution not based on love is senseless. Only the Woman† in *Masse Mensch*, who loves individuals, really loves the masses. The revolution which breaks out is soon on the verge of failure. Then the question of shooting bourgeois captives arises, an episode based directly on Toller's Munich experience. *Masse Mensch* is written in highly stylized language, with frequent omission of articles, contorted word order, etc. Thus a chorus chants: 'Wann werden Liebe wir leben?' This 'telegram style' seems to derive from Kaiser or Sternheim. At times Toller parodies official jargon.

After *Die Maschinenstürmer*, a play devoted to the Luddite riots, Toller wrote his crassest drama, *Hinkemann* (1924). As his name implies, Hinkemann is miserably crippled: he has lost his sex in the

---

* His name means, roughly, 'prince of peace.'
† All characters are nameless.

war, and all hope and faith in man as well; he believes that all the lessons taught by the recent catastrophes have been forgotten. Man will never change, he feels, and Toller, a fierce satirist here, seems to agree. Behind the smooth front of the Weimar state, cruelty and garish vulgarity prevail.—In *Hoppla, wir leben!*, his last important play (1927), Toller is even more pessimistic.

It has often been charged that Toller was a mere propagandist, not an artist. There are of course much declamation and loud moralizing in his dramas, but also scenes of great power. After all, in desperate times, the expressionistic scream may be the appropriate response.

Supposedly Thomas Mann once remarked: 'Bertolt Brecht is very talented—unfortunately.' The Naughty Brat attitude of Brecht's early career inevitably evoked such a reaction. While his concern with shocking the burghers, bragging of his sexual and alcoholic feats, and so on, is a venial sin, the prevalence in his works of hatred, malice, and nastiness is more disturbing, and recalls Toller's statement that one cannot love 'the masses' without loving individuals. Yet Brecht's anger, directed at sentimental German 'inwardness' as well as at social injustice, is largely justified. Beneath the façade of amoralism he was a moralist, and might even have liked to be friendly to people if the times permitted, as he claimed in a later poem. Similarly, a lyric stratum underlies the satiric surface of many of his works.

This lyric note is the most appealing aspect of his first drama, *Baal* (1922). Completely amoral, a cynical vagabond, Baal is also a genuine poet. He accepts all sides of life, especially those which seem wicked, forbidden, or dirty to the bourgeoisie. His fatalism is offset by a tremendous egotistic faith in himself. Like Gide's Prometheus, he devours the creature who would gnaw on him:

> Manchmal stellt sich Baal tot. Stürzt ein Geier drauf
> Speist Baal einen Geier, stumm, zum Abendmahl.

Brecht's next play, the abrasively bitter *Trommeln in der Nacht*, he ironically styled a comedy. To a point, the term may be defended: Brecht implies no empathy for his characters, and the placards hung in the theatre, like 'Glotzt nicht so romantisch'—Don't stare so romantically—command the audience to assume the same attitude.

(This is one of the earliest examples—there are others in the text—of Brecht's famous *Verfremdungseffekt*:* the spectators must be cooled down, admonished not to feel, but to think.)

In any case, one can hardly find that the fortunes of the protagonist Andreas Kragler are comic. Returned to Berlin from the war, he discovers that his fiancée has become the mistress of a profiteer; he forgives her and wins her back. That he belies his proletarian sympathies by refusing to join in the Spartacist revolt which has just broken out is regrettable, but we cannot condemn him, for like some of Hemingway's characters, he has taken as much punishment as he can.

Im Dickicht der Städte is set in a largely fictitious Chicago mainly peopled with criminals and their hangers-on. Precisely the rough and tough quality of the Chicago myth appealed to Brecht. The completely unmotivated feud between the Malayan Shlink and the clerk Garga is central in the action: life in the 'thicket' is absurd as well as dangerous. The language is hectically intense; Brecht admitted a debt to Rimbaud's *Une Saison en enfer*. Of course Brecht deliberately stylized American life: his Chicago is a metaphor of a fierce, amoral, crude, yet fascinating existence.

Since the novel normally calls for verisimilitude, and usually includes calm scenes and 'retarding elements,' one might expect that expressionistic writers would avoid it. Such is not the case, however: Döblin, Barlach, H. H. Jahnn, Werfel, Leonhard Frank, and lesser figures all cultivated it; and some of the novels of writers not primarily associated with the school—Heinrich Mann, Hesse and Wassermann come to mind—are clearly expressionistic.† Broadly, these works, like the comparable ones in other genres, emphasize motion and emotion, 'heightening' of the data normally provided by the senses, and the 'daemonic,' fantastic, and grotesque.

Yet there are variations: the visionary, as in much of Döblin, vs. the relatively realistic, as in Heinrich Mann. If one questions calling the latter an expressionist at all, the answer is that in his works of the Twenties he speeds up the action, strips away mere appearance to lay

* See below, pp. 135–138, where the later major works of Brecht (1898–1956) are discussed.

† Kafka's narratives, though sometimes labelled expressionistic, are usually precise and carefully controlled. See pp. 84–94.

bare underlying reality, and scorns 'common-sense' motivation. Thus he does intensify, 'ex-press,' besides sharing the radical ethics of the younger men. Further, there is a division between those whose aim is primarily a moral one—the title of Leonhard Frank's collection of stories, *Der Mensch ist gut*—is symptomatic, and those who care mainly for the daemonic, like Kasimir Edschmid and Klabund.

Clearly, the novella and sketch are more suited to the expressionistic temperament. Their novels tend to resemble a 'river without banks'—to cite the metaphoric title of a novel of Jahnn's, itself some 2,000 pages long. Several of Döblin's novels are marred by a similar lack of bounds, as is even Kafka's *Das Schloss*. In the shorter narrative, however, as in some of the stories of Sternheim and Döblin, the expressionists often achieved striking effects.

Seespeck and *Der gestohlene Mond*, Barlach's two novels, have much in common with his dramas: startling images, a sense of life as torture, a grotesque humour reminiscent of Jean Paul. Both have autobiographical elements; his *Ein selbsterzähltes Leben* (1928) is perhaps his most interesting prose work.

By no means a major figure, Kasimir Edschmid (i.e., Eduard Schmid, b. 1890) is historically important as a pioneer of expressionism both in his literary manifestos* and the early narratives collected in his volumes *Die sechs Mündungen* (1915) and *Das rasende Leben* (1916). As the latter title implies, Edschmid loved extreme situations—and exotic scenes as well.† Violence, cruelty, and perfervid eroticism abound. His style has been called visionary—see the Dionysiac dream in his novella 'Traum'—but like other expressionists he often marred his effects by overindulgence in abstract terms.

Like his dramas, Carl Sternheim's stories are marked by drastic satire against bourgeois attitudes and romantic illusions. Only a person who has seen through such illusions is free, but this liberation, at whatever cost, is priceless. Thus the policeman Busekow, in the novella of that name, finds escape from a world of drab routine in his passion for a prostitute. The French cook who is the protagonist of 'Napoleon,' an artist in his métier, gains saving insight into society by sceptically observing the customers in his excellent restaurants. The bourgeoisie who come to power after 1870 make him a misan-

---

* See above, p. 59.

† He has written several successful books about his travels.

thrope for a while, but he dies serenely. (Both these stories were included in *Die drei Erzählungen*, 1916.) In 'Ulrike' (1918), the sixteen-year-old daughter of a rigidly conventional, stiffly Protestant Prussian Junker leaves her home to become a nurse in the war. Its horrors finally open her naïve eyes: she breaks the ties of family and convention to become the mistress of an ultra-bohemian artist. Although Sternheim's style is less 'telegraphic' here than in his comedies, he uses starkly concentrated language, as in the following evocation of a scene in East Prussia: Von Blei schien meist der Himmel. Blaue Fahnen klafften kaum hinein, häufig aber strich Regen schräg und mengte aus Erde klebriges Gelb. . . .

In his expressionistic works, Alfred Döblin (b. 1878) combines the fantastic and the moral. At his best, as in *Berlin Alexanderplatz* (1929), there is a naturalistic element as well; *Ulysses*, *Doktor Faustus*, or for that matter *Faust*, are evidence that 'heightened' notes can well be included in the same work with realistic ones. I cannot include here the very moving story of Döblin's long journey from Berlin, through exile—he was Jewish, but would hardly have lived under Nazism in any case—in Russia and back to West Germany; from socialism to a Catholicism anything but reactionary. Avoiding the 'O Mensch!' pose of many expressionists, he has produced genuinely humane works.

Döblin's curiously entitled *Die Ermordung einer Butterblume*, a collection of short stories, appeared in 1913. The 'title story' is comparable to D. H. Lawrence's 'The Fox.' While it ostensibly describes only the decapitation of a flower, the sensitive reader feels at once that this murder reveals a Mephistophelean hatred of all life. Appropriately—from the expressionistic point of view—the diabolic murderer is a businessman. However tendentious, this is a brilliant story, but it was *Die drei Sprünge* des Wang-Lun*, a long novel published two years later, which made Döblin well known. Although based on an historical incident,[19] this religious *Bildungsroman* is highly expressionistic in its stress on inner states, its bold imagery, and its insistence that weakness, passivity, and resignation are far better than activity. (At the same time, Döblin includes an extraordinary number of sanguinary incidents.) 'Eingekellerte Augen';

---

* These *Sprünge*—one thinks of the 'leap of faith'—represent the three cardinal decisions of Wang-Lun's life.

'Die Karrees . . . finsterten' and hundreds of similar expressions give the desired intensity. As the leader of the 'Truly Weak Ones,' who have seceded from society and live like religiously oriented beatniks, Wang-Lun learns that the Chinese establishment will not tolerate such gestures; his whole group is finally exterminated. The application of Döblin's extended fable to the contemporary world is obvious.

Another of Döblin's novels, *Berge, Meere und Giganten*, deserves mention as one of the anti-Utopias characteristic of a troubled age.— *Berlin Alexanderplatz*, however, is generally thought to be his masterpiece. The novel has two heroes: Franz Biberkopf, a rather likeable, none too bright proletarian, and contemporary Berlin itself—tense, garish, often cruel, but with a saving wit and unexpected humaneness. Endowed with a large share of original sin—the novel has been called Döblin's first Christian work—Biberkopf learns by painful experience that 'letting oneself go' and selfishness have dire results, especially when one is an associate of criminals.

Obvious enough; but Döblin's language and evocation of metropolitan life are not. In technique he learned much from Dos Passos'* *Manhattan Transfer*, but he goes far beyond the American's ingenious reportage, inserting dramatic and even lyric elements, playing freely on words, introducing the leitmotif, and intervening to address his readers directly. Not quite a great novel, *Berlin Alexanderplatz* remains Döblin's most challenging book.

Although Gottfried Benn (1886–1956) was mainly known during the first part of his career for his provocative lyrics,† he was also a master of expressionistic prose. He published little fiction, turning to the essay in the Twenties, but his short volume of novellas, *Gehirne* (1916), is one of the memorable products of the movement.

These stories present the life, above all the thoughts, impressions, and self-doubts of Dr. Rönne, a brain surgeon. Clearly autobiographical, they are set in and around occupied Brussels, where Benn spent some three years as an army doctor. These brief novellas (or sketches?) express in short, nervous sentences Rönne's sense of isolation—communication seems impossible—and his belief that spirit

---

* He has denied any Joycean influence, but is at least indirectly indebted to *Ulysses*.

† See pp. 130–133.

and reality are absolutely cut off from one another. The story 'Die Eroberung' has as its climax the point that a man cannot 'conquer' another human being, let alone a city. Rönne's aim is to find clear, clean, logical answers, but all he discovers is—nothingness. (The Nietzschean theme of nihilism pervades most of Benn's work.) The cool, non-exclamatory expression of the style is perfectly fitted to the mood. Occasionally, brief evocations of beauty reveal Benn as a lyricist *malgré lui*.

The most extreme of the later expressionists, Hans Henny Jahnn (1894–1959) had considerable though not overwhelming talent as a dramatist and novelist (as well as an organ-builder and horse-breeder). Repugnant though his preoccupation with homosexuality, sadism, and bestiality is, he cannot be ignored. A 'northern pagan,' he believed in the superiority of all things Scandinavian; but this aberration did not lead him into Nazism. *Perrudja* (1929) is a strange, Utopian *Bildungsroman*, indebted to Joyce as well as to the expressionistic tradition.

Superficially, expressionism might be regarded as yet another 'ism' which held the stage for a decade or two and then vanished, another 'youth movement' which prematurely aged. Actually its thrust toward the greatest possible freedom for the artist's creative subjectivity and toward radical experimentation in style, metre, and stage techniques has had a permanent effect on later writers. Some may believe that the impact of expressionism has led more to disintegration than to liberation. It has cut both ways in its influence on its heirs, surrealism and the 'theatre of the absurd.' As one might expect, writers like Barlach, who did not hew close to the 'line,' are generally more interesting than the orthodox expressionists; and the stronger talents, men like Brecht and Benn, outgrew the movement. One hundred and fifty years earlier, when that very expressionistic school, the 'Storm and Stress,' collapsed, its more authentic poets similarly went on to other tasks.

6   *The Novel and Novella, 1918-1945**

... ob es nicht aussähe, als käme auf dem Gebiet des Romans heute
nur noch das in Betracht, was kein Roman mehr sei.

—*Thomas Mann*

No one who has written in German in the twentieth century has had
a greater impact on European literature than did Franz Kafka (1883–
1924). It is not merely that his style and choice of themes have affected the narrative in western Europe and the United States; though
he never wrote a play, his impact on the drama has been at least
equally great. The 'theatre of the absurd' would seem almost un-
thinkable without the example of Kafka's fiction.

Kafka spent most of his life in Prague, a hauntingly beautiful city,
yet one with dark, sinister quarters. As a member of a minority
within a minority, he was doubly isolated there. Suspicion and
hostility often divided speakers of German from the Czech majority,
and as a Jew, he was exposed to the anti-Semitic resentments common in the Austro-Hungarian Empire. He did not share the orthodox Jewish belief, yet disliked liberal Judaism. Still more crucial was
his relation to his vigorous, successful, and rather crude father; he
thought him an arbitrary tyrant, but instinctively felt that he was
right. ('Father figures,' some of them with religious overtones, are
everywhere in Kafka's fiction, notably so in 'Das Urteil.') Life
appeared to him as a series of insoluble dilemmas: he believed that
his position in the state insurance bureau was destroying his career
but that he must not resign; he felt guilty for remaining a bachelor
but still worse when faced with the possibility of marriage. While
still in his thirties, he contracted the tuberculosis of which he finally
died. Although he had devoted friends, was attractive to women,
and did not have to worry about money, his life, on balance, was
unusually grim.

* Some works published after 1945 but written by already well-established
novelists are included in this chapter.

Like Aesop's fables or Biblical parables, a representative work of Kafka's can be legitimately read in several different ways; usually there is a clearly autobiographical aspect; some narratives have religious or other overtones; at least one ('Josefine, die Sängerin oder das Volk der Mäuse') refers to the situation of the Jews. Thus there is no single 'secret key'; his novellas are like complicated equations in which any of several values may be assigned to 'x.' Basically, though, what he writes about is the human condition: thus Josef K., in *Der Prozess*, is primarily a man of a certain type, suddenly faced by a crisis.

Such an irruption of danger or disaster is a major theme of Kafka's. Small wonder that in virtually every one of his fictions fear, or irrational anxiety, or both, figures importantly. Other themes include the impossibility of communication, as in 'Beim Bau der chinesischen Mauer' and the closely related notion of incommensurability: thus there are no clear standards for judging the officials.[1] Probably a major reason for his frequent use of animals as protagonists—a monstrous insect, a badger, a monkey, and so on—is that their minds are *not* accessible to the reader. Günther Anders has argued that Kafka liked to make points by completely reversing the normal or natural way of expression: instead e.g. of stating 'the artist hungers' he entitled a story 'The Hunger Artist.'[2] This device, suggesting a most sensitive ear for nuances of speech, recalls his occasional puns: thus a monkey speaks of his 'äffisches Vorleben' and the word *Prozess* is once used to suggest a tubercular 'process' as well as a lawsuit. Like Hölderlin he deplored compulsive slavery to one's job or profession and the attendant loss of humane rationality. When asked why he is beating the emissaries of the court, in *Der Prozess*, the whipper replies: 'Zum Prügeln bin ich angestellt, also prügle ich'—anticipating the position taken by tens of thousands during the Nazi period. Another frequently sounded note is the implication that sexual love is degrading: the eternal feminine draws us downwards. And his caricature of the Austro-Bohemian bureaucracy affords comic relief at times.

These few themes Kafka repeats and varies brilliantly and forcefully. No one could claim that his range is large; what he generally presents, to be reductive, is the father complex in the atmosphere of a decaying society. He can remind one of the courtier in Goethe's

'Ilmenau,' who 'sings a monotonous song with great fervour.' Against this, Kafka's champions can well urge the power and focused 'purity' of his work. But what a small, airless world he shows us! It would be unfair to compare it with the creations of novelists who lived in more spacious times, but it is cramped indeed compared to that of Malraux, Mann, Sholokhov, or even Hesse. Yet of course this constriction is one of his main themes.

Often Kafka is included among the expressionists. This is plausible in terms of theme, imagery, and the urge to state existential situations in violent metaphors. Since however his language is notable for clarity and precision—his difficulty does not reside in his style—the label does not fit. While the expressionists shouted, Kafka wrote prose full of 'ifs' and subjunctives—the syntax of ambivalence. Instead of simplistic emotional outbursts à la Unruh or Toller, Kafka gives us careful, long-drawn-out analyses of motives and situations; in *Das Schloss*, this becomes downright painful. He had too much self-doubt, balance, and irony to use the modish rhetoric of his time.

The best of Kafka's novellas have an unsurpassed power and fascination. To discuss a few representative ones: 'Das Urteil' shows the clash between weak son and patriarchal father; the situation is expressionistic, but Kafka reverses the outcome: the father is victorious. As often in his stories (and in life) one cannot be sure which party is more in the right. While the father is near senility, he has moral authority over his son, who meekly commits suicide when his sire condemns him. Edmund Wilson has rightly complained of Kafka's weak, 'little boy' attitude towards familial or other authorities. No one who has read Kafka's long letter to his father (1919) can doubt that he was thinking of his own situation. Perhaps he could not have survived without transforming his problems into art.

'Die Verwandlung' (1916) is Kafka's most renowned novella. Few situations in literature are more frightening than that of poor Gregor Samsa—his last name is a cipher for 'Kafka'—who awakes to find himself an unpleasant, oversized insect. His transformation means in effect the renewed power of his father; as in 'Das Urteil,' an old man forcefully reasserts his rights. After gallant efforts to adjust himself to the new situation, Gregor dies. (A symbolic apple hurled at him by his father has putrefied in his body and contributed to his death.) We sympathize with his sufferings but also understand his family's relief at his death. Even his sister, who was particularly close to him, has come to feel that Gregor must disappear. As in 'Der Hungerkünstler' the healthy realists survive; the outsiders, however sensitive and gifted, succumb. Whether interpreted psychologically, religiously, or otherwise, the novella conveys the sense of burning inferiority and utter rejection.

'In der Strafkolonie'[3] is one of the most frightening and effective of all of Kafka's stories. The symbol of the harsh old order is the torture machine, designed by the 'Old Commander' ages before, an ingenious instrument which writes or rather tattoes the culprit's sentence on his body; the idiom *auf den Leib schreiben* is taken literally. During the twelve hours' punishment the condemned man comes to accept his fate; just before death, he experiences a moment of insight. Thus the machine 'works,' but the liberal conscience is revolting against it.

When the Explorer, a European, comes to the colony, he observes the punishment of a simple-minded soldier, condemned to death for disrespect. There has been no trial; as in *Der Prozess*, guilt is axiomatic. When asked his opinion by the Officer in charge, the Explorer rather reluctantly finds the proceedings unjust. As honest as he is reactionary—he had held absolute faith in the efficacy and justice of the machine—the Officer frees the prisoner and takes his place. At this the machine runs amok; instead of following its routine it flails about; there is no ritual killing: the Officer is brutally slaughtered. Yet when the Explorer leaves, he refuses to take the former prisoner along, and there are hints that the old order will return.

Basically this is a parable of two worlds, one dead, the other powerless even after birth. The archaic system functioned and was respected, while the new order seems wishy-washy and feminized. We are all condemned to death, and we gain insight—too late!— only through suffering; and in his darker hours, Kafka experienced life itself as a torture machine.

Even blacker in tone is 'Ein Landarzt.' One of Kafka's most nearly expressionistic stories, the narrative pours out at top speed, in a single paragraph. It is a nightmare world, in which the rules of time and space are magically suspended. The suspension of logic and probability is even more nightmarish: steeds emerge from a pig-sty, the patient at first has no wound but then reveals a horrible one, 'Rose' denotes both the doctor's servant—whose meaning for himself he realizes too late—and the wound itself. Again the irruption of disaster: once the doctor obeys the summons of the night bell—as is his duty—he is lost. As in 'In der Strafkolonie' two eras conflict; the doctor no longer has the *mana* of a medicine man, but rational science alone is inadequate. At the end, he is doomed to wander endlessly in a 'desert of ice,' 'naked and afraid,' in this Siberian landscape.

By no means evil, the doctor lacks force and decisiveness; he has never faced his own emotions, and fails equally in his professional life. And his fate seems a typical one in this 'most wretched of times.'

'Josefine die Sängerin, oder das Volk der Mäuse,' a humorous, almost light fable, was written in Kafka's last, relatively happy years (pub. 1924); he was dying, but had finally freed himself from his father. Basically, it is an ironic parable of the artist and his audience. 'Is Josefine really gifted? Does she deserve economic support?' the narrator, a representative bourgeois mouse, wonders. The answer is negative; but her concerts serve to give the mice a sense of solidarity. (Probably the mice also represent the Jewish people—terrified and oppressed, but somehow surviving and wryly enjoying life.) From the point of view of the ordinary mouse, Josefine is annoyingly temperamental, especially so since her talent is slight, but she is accepted. The style, with its plays on the key-word *pfeifen*—she pipes or whistles, unable really to sing—has surprising gaiety.

Kafka never finished a novel, but his best long narrative, *Der Prozess* (1925), came much closer to completion than the others. Actually, as he left instructions to destroy all his unpublished works and fragments, he was apparently dubious about the quality of all three; the others are *Das Schloss* (1926) and *Amerika* (1927). Fortunately his faithful friend Max Brod disregarded his request.*

In its imperfect state, *Amerika* is even more enigmatic than Kafka's works usually are. Even the title, another of Brod's contributions, is a misnomer;[4] Kafka himself referred to it as 'Der Verschollene,' implying an unhappy outcome, but he himself was unsure how to end the book. If one takes the chapter 'Das Naturtheater von Oklahoma' literally and follows Brod in making it the last one,[5]

* *Amerika*, published last, was begun first (1912), *Der Prozess* was started in 1914, *Das Schloss* some time later.

the novel appears as a *Bildungsroman*, with Karl as a twentieth-century Parzival or Green Henry. Kafka's warmly acknowledged debt to Dickens also points in this direction. Probably the best reading of the novel as it stands is that it ends on a mildly ironic note, more happy than sad.

Karl Rossmann, its sixteen-year-old protagonist, emigrates to America perforce: his father banished him because he was seduced by a servant girl. Such passivity is typical in Kafka's stories, and Karl remains naïve and rather weak, though well-meaning. The first chapter (published separately as 'Der Heizer' in 1913) makes his character very clear. When about to disembark in New York, he falls in with a stoker who protests, rightly or wrongly, that he is the victim of gross injustice. Karl impulsively rushes with him to the Captain's cabin, a trial is held, but the stoker proves ineffective and rather unprepossessing. Only the appearance of his rich Uncle Jacob saves Karl from grave embarrassment. Karl has wanted justice but actually has increased the proletarian's troubles. Regretfully but finally he abandons the stoker.

The chasm separating rich and poor in the United States is a repeated theme. Even more important is the gap between appearance and reality, between the myth of America and American life. In describing the harbour and the ship, Kafka introduces various distortions, the most striking of which being that the Statue of Liberty holds not a torch but a sword: things are harsher than the emigrants had been led to expect. Furthermore, life in the States is marked by unpredictable, often dangerous, shifts of fortune. Professor Politzer, however, is clearly right in maintaining that Kafka was not directing a satire against America; there is no hint that life in Europe is easier or better.

This mercurial quality is paralleled by Uncle Jacob's fickleness. He rejects Karl on a feeble pretext, and the youth goes 'on the road,' falling in with some sinister persons but also with some kind ones, and discovering a further rough side of American life while doing menial work in a hotel.

Eventually he arrives at the 'Nature Theatre of Oklahoma,' where he meets a cherished friend, and finds work, even though he does not have proper credentials. The theatre is a fantastic institution in which everyone may find a role: women appear as angels, men as devils. (Europeans have long complained that Americans 'put women on a pedestal'; this happens literally in the 'Nature Theatre.') To quote the exclamatory but ambiguous placard advertising it:

> . . . The great theatre of Oklahoma calls you! It calls today only, once only! Whoever misses the chance will never get another! Whoever thinks of his future belongs in our ranks! Everyone is welcome! Whoever wants to be one of our artists should come forward! We are the theatre which can use everyone, each in his place! Whoever has decided to join us is to be congratulated right now! But hurry, so that you can be interviewed by midnight! At twelve everything will be closed for good! A curse on anyone who does not believe us! . . .

Obviously the theatre is a metaphor or symbol, and there are many interpretations. I would suggest that it represents the picture of America projected in Europe to attract immigrants—hence the bombastic style of the placard and its fierceness towards doubters. This image is radically different from Karl's experiences. Nevertheless, it is partly true: there is something, however bizarre, for everyone to do. And no one is the prisoner of bureaucracy.

'Some one must have slandered Josef K., for without his having done anything bad, he was arrested one morning.' Thus *Der Prozess* begins, *in medias res* like 'Die Verwandlung.' Typically, punishment precedes guilt, or at least is apparent before any offence becomes evident. Like the other agents of the Court, the men who arrest him are ambiguous figures, quite unrelated to the regular police. They do not take him to a judge but grant him an illusory freedom, like that of a dog on a long chain.

We note, however, that though the narrative is told in the third person, we see things through Josef's eyes. His uncle, the priest in the cathedral scene, and others have very different viewpoints. Josef is a bachelor (a state which Kafka always denigrated), thirty years old, who has a good position in a bank and seems completely 'normal.' Gradually we learn that his relations with women and his family are perfunctory and mechanical; he has no real friends. Thus when Josef makes advances to Fräulein Bürstner, a typist who has a room in the same lodging house, his wooing is so clumsy and tactless that one wonders if he is capable of love; he is neither hot nor cold.

The next Sunday Josef goes to the Court; some mysterious force seems to guide him. It is located in sordid rooms in a shabby part of the city (obviously Prague). Its servants, like the judges, are dubious if not corrupt; as often in the novel, a sense of airlessness and an aura of illicit sexuality surrounds it.[6] Certainly this is an expression and symbol of *Angst*. Its quarters are labyrinthine (among other things it is a vast, and very Austrian, bureaucracy) but there is no thread of Ariadne.

Gradually the impact of this intangible threat shakes Josef's self-confidence. His career at the bank suffers, and when his uncle hears of it, he insists on consulting an advocate, Dr. Huld.* Typically, Josef vitiates what slight 'grace' this might bring: he makes love, joylessly, to the lawyer's web-fingered assistant, Leni—a not completely human female—thus annoying the lawyer. A second episode, with the court painter Titorelli, is even more squalid.

The chapter 'In the Cathedral' brings the climax. Already close to a breakdown, Josef K. is directed by his chief to meet an Italian business man and 'show him the sights.' The Italian does not appear, but in the dark cathedral a priest suddenly thunders out his name. After reproaching and warning him, he tells him the parable 'Before the Law.'[7]

Here a 'man from the country'† tries to enter an opening in the wall which confronts him. The doorkeeper prevents him; the man spends the rest of his life before the hole, frightened by the things he has been told about even more powerful doorkeepers but still pathetically eager to enter. Just before he dies the doorkeeper informs him, cruelly enough, that this entrance had been meant for him alone; he will now close it.

Clearly, the 'man from the country' is a miniature Josef K., who somehow cannot 'get through.' There have been endless discussions about where the guilt lies, what the doorkeeper symbolizes, etc.; in fact, Josef and the priest discuss the matter at length. A few things are evident: like Josef, the simpleton errs in neglecting to ask what the trouble is and in failing to risk everything for his salvation.[8] (There is of course no guarantee that he would have succeeded even

---

* *Huld* means 'Grace'—divine or otherwise. No orthodox believer, Kafka is presumably ironic here.

† A Hebrew euphemism for an ignoramus.

then.) Dismissing Josef, the priest says that the law wants nothing from him and will neither pursue nor detain him—an obvious untruth.[9]

In the last chapter, two grotesque executioners dressed in black come for Josef K. He sarcastically describes them as 'tenors'—too late, he firmly opposes the Court. Although his last words are 'like a dog' he does die like a man, refusing to ease the executioners' assignment by killing himself. Just before death, he sees a lighted window, and thinks he sees Fräulein Bürstner; but the attempt to interpret his end as somehow triumphant is pitiable.

To venture an interpretation: *Der Prozess* indicates that we are all condemned to death—there is no recorded case of the Court's acquitting anyone—to original sin (at least to the *crimen individuationis*)[10]—and to unhappiness. Josef's basic guilt is simply that he is mortal; but beyond that he has never loved, never really lived. The Court itself is at least equally guilty.

Other readings include the theological—the Court is divine, all the more so since it is incommensurable;* the largely plausible interpretation that it represents the unconscious; the farfetched notion that it is a symbol of fascism; that it satirizes Austro-Bohemian bureaucracy; the point—correct but peripheral—that the word *Prozess* has reference to Kafka's tubercular 'process.' In most of these theories there is some truth, but essentially *Der Prozess* is yet another parable of an average man in a state of crisis, and of his defeat.

Kafka's longest novel, *Das Schloss*, is considerably less complete than *Der Prozess*, and thus more difficult to grasp. An outsider, 'K,' comes on a dark, wintry day to a village dominated by a mysterious castle. The rest of the book deals—for some 500 pages—with his efforts to enter it. More aggressive than Josef K., often clumsily so, he is at least no miserable wretch like the protagonists of 'Das Urteil' and 'Die Verwandlung.' Presumably he would have been allowed finally to settle down in the village, but never to gain admittance to the castle itself.

The book is a series of ambiguities and contradictions; Kafka seemed to take a dour pleasure in expressing confusion and frustration. We cannot be sure that K. tells the truth about his past or is

---

* More logically, one could consider it diabolic, or at least evil. See Erich Heller, *The Disinherited Mind* (Philadelphia, 1952), pp. 176f.

really trained to be a surveyor. The officials of the castle are especially enigmatic: practically every rumour about them conflicts with an opposite one. The identity of Klamm, the bureaucrat especially charged with the case, remains most unclear; perhaps he does not even exist. Similarly, we do not know whether the lord of the establishment, Count Westwest, is good or evil or represents death, life, or neither.

Thus the villagers, who live the humble life of ordinary people, do not attempt to judge the class which lives, in several senses, above them. Like Schnitzler's aristocrats, the officials habitually choose mistresses from the lower class. Only one girl has ever refused, Amalia: after her revolutionary act, she grimly endures the bleak life of an outsider.

The labyrinthine[11] castle, of continually shifting appearance, clearly symbolizes a reality which men cannot understand. The strange telephone connection between castle and village—one can never be sure to whom one is talking, or if the invisible partner is telling the truth—makes the same point, rather on the comic level: the image has reference to Austrian reality as well as to metaphysics.

As the book further follows K.'s endless attempts to force his way to his goal, it, like him, begins to 'go around in circles.' His desperate devices, attempts at influencing the officials through third persons,* and above all the logomachy about the true nature of the castle, become monotonous. Towards the end, K. seems on the verge of success. He surprises a castle official at night, off his guard; the bureaucrat seems actually to love him, to be ready to fulfil his every wish. Then K., snatching defeat from the jaws of apparent victory, falls asleep and forfeits his chance. Politzer shows persuasively that the official deliberately lured him to sleep.[12]

Such behaviour reminds one of Professor Heller's argument that the Castle, far from being the incarnation of divine law and Grace as Brod thought it, is inhabited by Gnostic demons.[13] Again though, we cannot judge: we know the officials only through the confused perceptions of K. and the villagers. We can say that it is an expression of 'the other,' that it is undoubtedly real, but that in life at least, we

---

* Like Josef K., he 'depends too much on women.' He has won Frieda, a former mistress of Klamm, but the *coup* brings him neither advantage nor happiness.

shall never understand it: it is by definition as inaccessible as Kant's *Ding an sich*. In an aphorism about his own works, Kafka wrote: 'All of these parables (or metaphors: *Gleichnisse*) wish only to convey that the incomprehensible cannot be comprehended; and that we knew already.' *Ignorabimus!*

Wolfgang Kayser once remarked: 'Kafka is an illness'; and indeed his writings, if accepted as ultimate interpretations of reality, can function as powerful depressants. (As Camus' reaction showed, however, they may act as a spur to a resolutely existentialist attitude.) Yet he was not only a true artist but a man from whose vision of life as illness we learn much about the human condition.

In 1924, two years before *Das Schloss* appeared, Thomas Mann published an even more ambitious novel, *Der Zauberberg*. Monumental in scope, this inexhaustible book can be approached in a number of ways. It is a *Bildungsroman* concerning the education of the 'simple' but potentially brilliant Hans Castorp, who may also be regarded as a representative young German of his time, or even an Everyman. Affected by the malaise typical of his time, Castorp develops a—rather mild—case of tuberculosis; his convalescence takes seven years, largely spent in intellectual and spiritual explorations. (It is typical that almost all his adventures take place in the realm of the mind.) Also, *Der Zauberberg* is a *Zeitroman* in a triple sense: it describes a time (1907–14), discusses time, and time is itself a major force in the action. Politically, it deals with Germany, the 'middle kingdom' between West and East; philosophically with the conflict between reason and instinct, light and dark, life and death. One of its most rewarding aspects is its humour: it abounds in plays on words, and in realistic detail, amusing or grotesque: the malapropisms of Frau Stöhr, the girl who whistles through her pneumothorax, the corpses sent down to the valley on a bobsled, are unforgettable. At the other end of the spectrum it appears as a mythical novel of a questing hero[14] who sets out to seek adventures, wins the love of an enchantress, passes through ordeals, etc.

Contrary to widespread opinion, *Der Zauberberg* is not a 'heavy' novel: it deals in part with ideas but also offers jokes, ironies, and a cast of 'real people.' One cannot but sense the magnetism of Clavdia, the Dionysiac appeal of Peeperkorn, the charm of the wordy Settembrini, the mordant wit of Naphta, the courage of Joachim, the excitement of the carnival. Lesser figures, like the ambiguous Behrens and the still more dubious psychoanalyst Krokowski, add to the richness of the book. At least four 'set pieces' stand out: the carnival, a veritable Walpurgis Night; the snowstorm in which Castorp, literally lost, briefly finds himself intellectually; the 'last supper' which the alcoholic Peeperkorn gives his followers; and the spiritualistic séance at which the ghost of Joachim appears, ominously, in the helmet and grey uniform worn by German soldiers in the First World War.

Paradoxically, it is as a philosophical novel that *Der Zauberberg* is somewhat disappointing. Although Castorp learns a great deal from the long, often coruscating debates between Settembrini, the champion of reason and life and Naphta, the brilliant representative of the non-rational forces, he does not achieve a permanent resolution. To be sure, he perceives in his magnificent vision in the snow that he must overcome the 'romantic' fascination with death which had previously dominated his life 'for the sake of goodness and love.' Yet he soon forgets the purpose of his epiphany, and lingers on for years on the enchanted mountain. Moreover, though he has learned to champion love against death, it is the outbreak of war which frees him; he goes to the front. The last words of the novel express the hope that love will reassert itself finally: rather cold comfort.

The two novellas which Mann wrote during the Twenties deserve mention. *Unordnung und frühes Leid*, published two years after the pedagogical novel, is an affectionately ironic account of the relations between the generations in a German family. Located in the time of the inflation, it also implies guarded hopefulness about contemporary society.—Far more serious, *Mario und der Zauberer* (1930) presents a frightening symbolic picture of fascism. The hypnotist Cipolla,* fascinates his audiences by 'powers stronger than reason or virtue'; mere rationality cannot withstand him. Finally the simple Mario, whose human dignity Cipolla has outraged, brings him down.

Probably the most monumental work produced by an emigrant from Nazi Germany is Thomas Mann's tetralogy *Joseph und seine Brüder* (1933–43). The theme, chosen in the mid-Twenties, proved all too appropriate. Mann was forced to live in an alien land, and the

---

* He also represents a sinister sort of 'black' artist.

day when he could, if he chose, return to his erring brothers was approaching by the time the last words were published.

In *Joseph* Mann greatly expands the use of mythical, archetypal characters begun in *Der Tod in Venedig*. The basic myth is that of dying and rebirth, a consoling, even 'happy' belief. One can read *Joseph* as a *Bildungsroman* in which not only the hero but the Jewish people and even God himself develop; at the same time the modern consciousness grows out of the archaic way of thinking. Balancing the philosophic aspect is a picaresque one: Joseph is a sly, though benevolent and beneficent rogue. The book, like *Der Zauberberg* and *Doktor Faustus*, gives the semblance of great learning; Mann 'sweated up' much Egyptian mythological and Biblical lore.

'Myth' had become a favourite notion of reactionary intellectuals, including the fascist ones. Mann deliberately took over this fruitful concept from his enemies and made it serve a human and humane intention. Joseph develops towards the goal of a balance between spirit (*Geist*) and the emotions, symbolized by the 'double blessing.' He is too mundane for the religious blessing of Israel.

To make his myth viable as fiction, Mann widened the use of the leitmotif strikingly. In *Joseph* not only words and phrases, but typical situations appear and reappear: thus hostile brethren, he notes, recur from the 'time' of the Egyptian gods onward. This is in line with the psychology of his patriarchal characters—the initiated believe that time is an illusion—as well as with the Nietzschean doctrine of eternal return.

As the tetralogy approaches its 'happy ending,' the tone becomes increasingly light. It begins with the ominously titled prelude 'Höllenfahrt,' starting with the magnificent sentence: 'Tief ist der Brunnen der Vergangenheit,' but the Egypt of the Pharaohs appears as extremely modern. In describing it, Mann directed some good-natured irony at America. While the recognition scene is very moving, even here we see how Joseph, that consummate artist, has stage-managed the whole encounter.

Lotte in Weimar (1939) is the most significant of several works Mann wrote during the years when he was composing *Joseph*. Like the tetralogy it evinces his increasing fascination by myth. Without suppressing any of the difficult aspects of Goethe's personality, it shows him as a mythic character. Further, the idea of return, of timeless patterns is central. Lotte returns more than forty years after Goethe's passionate love for her; at the same time his love is repeated, mythically speaking, in his passion for a much younger woman.

The novel is a *montage* of hundreds, probably thousands of allusions to or quotations from Goethe's works, letters, etc. In this case no cramming was needed: Mann's knowledge of the poet was genuine and broad, and the result is an elaborate tapestry. He approaches the poet through a variety of points of view; each narrator sees an aspect of the truth, not always a pleasant one. In the seventh chapter—Mann made a fetish of this number—Goethe himself speaks in a long, brilliant interior monologue. The *montage* technique enables Mann to combine a number of quotations of the poet with his own imitation of him;[15] the continuous flow of Goethe's ideas from one subject to another is brilliantly rendered.

Much of the novel is concerned with the high cost of genius in human terms; Goethe's tends to sear the lives of his intimates; Lotte is shocked and disillusioned. At the end, the two are apparently reconciled, but actually Goethe 'returns' only in her hallucination. As often, Mann had his cake and ate it.

Doktor Faustus (1947) is Mann's most intense, difficult, and hotly debated book. Stirred to shame and anger by Nazism, Mann abandoned his usual ironic reserve: this work was to be as tragic as any of Dostoevsky's. Dealing with damnation and written mainly during the war, the book is doubly dark.

The aim of the book is both sublime and complex. Mann related the life of Leverkühn, a composer of genius. At the same time the 'Faustian' story of his achievements and damnation suggests both the situation of modern art and the degradation and fall of Germany. To reconcile these seemingly disparate ends Mann employed several themes and devices. Thus the 'lateness,' in Spengler's sense, of modern culture corresponds to the late emergence of Germany as a great power. Both are ready to use desperate means, even to sign a pact with evil, to 'break through.' Mann made his Faustus a musician, that being the national art. Leverkühn's life is largely modelled on Nietzsche's, whose ideas had done much to shape the attitudes of his countrymen. Finally, by using the fiction that the narrator, Serenus Zeitblom, is writing his life of Leverkühn during the Second World

War—he often interrupts the story to mention Nazi crimes or bombed cities—Mann linked the two 'times' more closely together.

One key to this most complicated work is the notion of the magic square, in which the numbers, on any level, 'add up' to the same result. Thus 'breaking through' applies to Adrian's own career, to the Germany of 1914 and 1933, to the condition of modern music (and literature), and to Mann's own ambitions in writing *Doktor Faustus*.

Adrian's breakthrough was the composition of 'Dr. Faustus' Lament,' a work in which the mathematical rigidity of his twelve-tone music is dialectically transmuted into extreme expressivity. Possibly Adrian's life will be justified by his work, despite his offences. Future generations, we are told, will draw health from his illness. His coldness and arrogance are perhaps only the armour of a fiercely ardent nature.

Believing that Mann had condemned their entire national tradition, many Germans fiercely resented *Doktor Faustus*. His indictment was indeed sweeping, but his anger rose from bitter disappointment. Zeitblom's words, the last of the book, evince compassion not hatred. 'Gott sei euerer armen Seele gnädig, mein Freund, mein Vaterland.'

Grace is in fact a major theme of the light, largely parodistic *Der Erwählte* (1951). Gregorius, the child of incest, and himself involuntarily incestuous, repents so intensely that he is purified. After seventeen years of self-imposed punishment, he is chosen pope, and proves to be a very great one. Throughout the tone is light; Mann plays with and on themes usually thought too serious for parody. The charm of *Der Erwählte* lies mainly in its language, with its puns, jests, deliberate weaving together of different languages, etc. It is 'an art-work in words'—*ein sprachliches Kunstwerk*.

Inevitably, the books Mann published soon after *Faustus* seemed anticlimactic. In *Felix Krull*,* however, he regained the level of his best work. Mann has always been a humorist, as his works from *Buddenbrooks* on attest; but difficulties of translation have tended to obscure this fact. An excerpt from this picaresque novel had been published over forty years earlier, but no sense of disunity mars the completed First Part. In the parts written last, there are more and

* Full title: *Bekenntnisse des Hochstaplers Felix Krull*, I (1954).

more references to myth, with Felix appearing as a modern Hermes, but this does not break the mood.

True to his name, Felix is a gay deceiver, who steals rather because that is his talent than for gain. Accordingly people, especially women, are fond of him; one lady expressly urges him to rob her. Of course he is crooked (*krull*) as well as felicific. Returning to his old theme that the artist deals only with semblances, Mann is no longer troubled by it but finds it a source of amusement, as Wedekind, in his boisterous way, had already done.

Mann's last published work was his brilliant 'Versuch über Schiller,' by far his finest essay, and possibly the best ever written on the dramatist. Mann died at eighty in the year the 'Versuch' appeared (1955), honoured throughout the world and apparently reconciled, like Joseph, with his once hostile nation.

Understandably but regrettably, Heinrich Mann's polemics against Hitler are too shrilly bitter even to be good propaganda, let alone literature. In his American exile—like his brother he spent a number of years in Southern California—he wrote his finest novels: *Die Jugend des Königs Henri Quatre* and its sequel *Die Vollendung des Königs Henri Quatre*. Elsewhere successful mainly as a satirist,* he has created here two portraits of a man he found truly admirable. Henri IV, after all, was witty, tolerant, amorous, unconcerned with dogmatic religion—and, not least, like most of Mann's literary heroes, he was a Frenchman. (In some ways, Henri is remarkably close to Thomas Mann's Joseph: the ideal ruler.) The novels are written in a clear, witty, and remarkably well-tempered prose; most unexpectedly, the tone is mellow.

In Mann's brilliant, semi-autobiographical work *Ein Zeitalter wird besichtigt*, he includes fascinating reminiscences about his own life, his brother, other authors, and the Weimar Republic generally; but also Stalinoid encomiums of the Soviet Union as a bastion of human freedom. This strange amalgam of insight and blindness is, alas, characteristic of Heinrich Mann.

To turn to another writer already well known before 1918, Hermann Hesse: his *Der Steppenwolf* (1927) is in action, theme, and style the most experimental—and the most successful—of his books.

* See above, pp. 48–50.

Like *Demian*, it is a reflection of his psychoanalysis; it too is a *Bildungsroman*. But here the hero's education is portrayed without any prettifications in the seemingly mad world of the 'magic theatre.' Hesse is able to cast a cold eye on his autobiographical protagonist, Harry Haller. We see him from the viewpoints of a 'well-adjusted' bourgeois, of the author of the satire 'Tract about the Steppenwolf,' and of the Steppenwolf himself. The tone has no longer the adolescent fervour of *Demian*: Haller is cut down to size, and made likeable. When he can laugh at himself and act out (symbolically) his aggressive feelings, he is well on the way to health. In the 'magic theatre' Hesse took up the Walpurgis Night metaphor, as Joyce, Mann, and lesser writers had done. Thus his Haller can shoot automobiles from ambush and commit sexual offences and even murder without causing any tangible damage.

At the same time, the 'magic theatre' is an image of the unconscious mind. Here Harry meets his '*anima*' Hermine; here the long-suppressed wishes of his Freudian id seem to have come true: 'Alle Frauen sind dein,' a placard tells him, and even perverted drives can be satisfied without shame. Not only is Haller a wolf as well as a man: he contains within his psyche Jungian archetypes of all sorts. Above all, he must learn, like Sinclair in *Demian*, not to take everything with such tense seriousness, not to judge himself and others so harshly. At the end he is 'sentenced' to eternal life; with a Nietzschean turn of phrase, he resolves to start the game of life once more.

Although it centres on a philosophical theme—Hesse's favourite notion of unity underlying polarity—*Narziss und Goldmund* is lighter in tone. A critic has well complained of the didacticism of the dialogue[16] between Narziss, the egoistic representative of spirit, and Goldmund, the protagonist of life, but elsewhere the book is downright gay, especially in recounting Goldmund's erotic triumphs.

Das Glasperlenspiel (1943) similarly contrasts polar characters. Here the career of the representative of the spirit, Joseph Knecht, is central. The bead game is a metaphor of intellectual activity carried on for its own sake: its players are dedicated monks of the mind. A protest against recent and contemporary barbarism, the long novel deals with the irreplaceable value, and the limitations, of pure intellect. (Knecht, the appropriately named *servus servorum Dei*, returns to the world at the end.) While the book deliberately avoids any depiction of violent actions or passions, it is by no means dull. Written in serene, transparent prose, it contains some of Hesse's best lyrics.

Although one of the most famous and successful of twentieth-century writers, Stefan Zweig (1881–1942) led an essentially melancholy life, and his work, judged by austere standards, is rather disappointing. Basically the cultivated European—Erasmus was one of his heroes—Zweig experienced the First War, the rise of Nazism, exile from Austria, and the outbreak of the second conflict. Early in 1942, when the Allied forces seemed to be losing, he committed suicide, writing in his farewell declaration that he no longer had the energy to persevere, 'after the world of my own language has, for me, perished [he was Jewish] and my spiritual home, Europe, is destroying itself.'

Zweig wrote a great deal, in several genres. While his novels are not distinguished, a few of his novellas are; all of them show skill and psychological subtlety. His two best-known collections are *Amok* and *Verwirrung der Gefühle*. Perhaps his finest novella is 'Die unsichtbare Sammlung,' dealing with a collector of rare books who has to sacrifice one after another during the inflation of the early Twenties merely to keep alive. Zweig's lyrics are derivative; his pacifist drama *Jeremias* (1917) shows genuine nobility but little theatrical flair. Perhaps his finest accomplishment is in the long historical essay. Zweig published a series of 'triptychs,' each dealing with three related figures, under the general title 'Baumeister der Welt.' Of these *Der Kampf mit dem Dämon* (1925), interpreting Hölderlin, Kleist, and Nietzsche, particularly reveals Zweig's insight and empathy. The most moving of his works is his autobiography *Die Welt von Gestern* (1942).

For several years after 1918 writers generally avoided the theme of the First War, feeling perhaps that the experience was still too traumatic to appeal. In the middle and late Twenties, though, a succession of war novels, some of them of remarkable quality, appeared.[17] While Ludwig Renn's *Krieg* and Erich Maria Remarque's *Im Westen Nichts Neues* scored the greatest popular successes, the finest of these works, by general agreement, is Arnold Zweig's *Der Streit um den Sergeanten Grischa* (1927).

Arnold Zweig began his career as a rather traditional novelist, primarily concerned with personal relationships among cultivated members of the middle class; his style in his earlier works, like *Novellen um Claudia*, is indebted to Thomas Mann's. Service at the front opened his eyes: he evolved into a socialist and an internationalist. Without caricature or oversimplification, he shows in the symbolic case of Grischa a struggle for justice involving the decent forces in the Prusso-German tradition against the far more brutal militarism of the 'new men' like Schieffenzahn (Ludendorff). When Grischa is executed, there is a profound sense of moral defeat, all the more since he is no martyr of the expressionist sort but very human. The odour and 'feel' of the forests of Eastern Europe are excellently rendered. Later Zweig devoted a whole cycle to the war years; the other novels are not of the same level, and those he wrote during exile and afterwards—he returned from Palestine to (East) Berlin in 1948—are monotonously subservient to the Marxist line.

Of the other war novels, Remarque's, while far better than the nationalist critics admitted, is hardly a work of art; Theodor Plievier's *Des Kaisers Kulis* strikingly evokes the life of ordinary seamen in the German navy, very much from the Left. Few of the war books written by partisans of the Right deserve mention, but those of the highly gifted Ernst Jünger are an exception. Much influenced by the late works of Nietzsche, he sees war as the great crucible in which man is tested and hardened; his *In Stahlgewittern* (1920) is impressive in a repulsive way; he writes strongly and cleanly. Hans Carossa's *Rumänisches Tagebuch* (1924) has no observable political overtones: it tells, with the objectivity of a physician but with a genuinely poetic talent, of the author's experiences at the front. Carossa's fiction and verse are rather parochial. Franz Werfel's (1890–1945) very voluminous work is no longer greatly esteemed, but some of it, particularly of his non-expressionistic prose, deserves respect. Here he successfully avoids his usual temptations: vagueness, sentimentality, and pseudo-profundity. The novel *Verdi* (1924) centres on the symbolic contrast between music in Bach's tradition, still clearly related to the human and the divine, to the demonic, 'mythic' music of Wagner. Perhaps only a citizen of the old 'Holy Roman Empire'—Werfel was born in Prague—could have drawn the distinction so clearly, without in any sense underrating Wagner's genius. Doubtless Werfel's finest novel is *Die vierzig Tage des Musa Dagh* (1933) in which he depicts the heroic self-defence of the Armenians against their Turkish persecutors. Presumably Werfel thought of his own long-oppressed people, the Jews, while writing *Musa Dagh*, though he can hardly have foreseen the atrocities to come. His last novel is the unconvincingly Utopian *Stern der Ungeborenen* (1946), in which he characteristically relapses into 'talking about' a subject rather than truly forming it.

Two minor talents of the time deserve mention. Hans Fallada (actually Rudolf Ditzen, 1893–1947) had a certain realistic gift: his underdog's perspective is honest if very limited. His *Kleiner Mann, Was Nun?* (1932) recounts the fate of a little man during the great depression, and is a civilian equivalent of *Im Westen Nichts Neues*.— More gifted, the parodist Erich Kästner (b. 1899) has not yet fulfilled his promise; during the Nazi period he supported himself mainly by writing children's books. Indeed, his reputation is based largely on 'juveniles' like *Emil und die Detektive* and such collections of satiric verse as *Herz auf Taille*. Yet he wrote, in *Fabian, die Geschichte eines Moralisten*, the *Werther* of the 1920's. Basically the 'pure fool,' Fabian undergoes numerous adventures, mainly disreputable, in the Berlin of those days. He dies trying to save a child from drowning, because (typically) 'er konnte leider nicht schwimmen.' Slight though it is, *Fabian* is an honest document of the disillusioned era of '*Neue Sachlichkeit*.'

While Robert Musil (1880–1942) was a well-known writer during his own life, his fame did not rest primarily on what is judged today his greatest book by far: *Der Mann ohne Eigenschaften*.* Rather, he was known for his early 'school novel' *Die Verwirrungen des Zöglings Törless* (1906), for two collections of experimental, often difficult novellas, two plays, and various essays, of which '*Über die Dummheit*' is the most brilliant. In 1938, when Hitler invaded Austria, Musil left voluntarily. His last years he spent in Zürich, where Büchner, Joyce, and many other literary exiles had found refuge.

Robert Edler von Musil was a rarity in modern German literature; he was as both keenly rational as say Valéry or Gide and as able to cope with the actual world as most businessmen. He was trained as an engineer and mathematician; then, planning an academic career like his father's, he studied logic and experimental psychology. (Signifi-

---

* Only part of the long work appeared during Musil's lifetime. (Vol. I, 1930; Vol. II, 1933).

cantly, his dissertation was devoted to the epistemology of the sceptic Ernst Mach.) The success of *Törless*, however, made him decide to be a writer.

This novel is typically Musilian in various ways. Unlike most works of its genre, it depicts the struggles of adolescents quite unsentimentally: Törless undergoes very unpleasant experiences, but survives. Musil's dry, ironic insight into character is already apparent, as in his readiness to deal honestly with unpleasant themes—in this case sadism.

Vereinigungen (1911) contains two novellas centred on sexual union, as the title implies, but free of any sensationalism. While they have been compared with impressionist paintings, these stories provide impressions of psychological states mainly; the visual world is evanescent and vague. In 'Die Vollendung der Liebe,' a woman is led, through adultery with an unloved stranger, to overcome resentment of her husband and perfect her love for him. However unconvincing this paradoxical development, it is presented with great skill. The three stories of *Drei Frauen* (1924) present women in precarious, exposed relationships with lovers of different nationality and, in two cases, of higher class than they. The 'death wish' plays an important part, but not in any romantic sense. Persons and scenes emerge much more clearly than in the earlier stories.

Paradoxically, *Der Mann ohne Eigenschaften* is a great book but not a successful work of art. Musil never could finish it; worse, the narrative loses all direction, like a once great river ending in stagnation. There is also needless repetitiousness.[18] Yet the novel's virtues are such that to read it is an experience.

Its opening paragraph is typical of Musil and his *alter ego*, the protagonist Ulrich:

> Over the Atlantic a barometric low prevailed; it moved eastward, towards a high located above Russia, . . . The isotherms and isotheres did their duty. The air temperature was properly related to the median annual temperature, to the temperature of the coldest as of the warmest month, and to aperiodic monthly variation. . . . To use an expression which describes the actual state of things quite well, even if it is somewhat old-fashioned: it was a fine August day of the year 1913.

Of course this is the approach of natural science; more important, beginning a work of fiction in this way is bold and witty. Indeed, wit is one of the book's greatest virtues. Musil's choice of names for his characters is unsurpassable: his hero calls a nymphomaniac mistress Bonadea; a silly bluestocking appears as Diotima; and a quiet, unintellectual but intelligent general bears the name Stumm von Bordwehr. Considering, like Karl Kraus, the corruption of language by journalism, Ulrich notes that a tennis player is called *genial* in the papers; why not then a 'racehorse of genius'?

How can Ulrich, largely an image of Musil, be 'without qualities'? Like Castorp, he finds the contemporary world unsatisfying. Men are losing all sense of identity. The old values no longer hold, for modern culture as a whole, including morality and theology, is as least a century behind natural science. Therefore Ulrich takes a year off to think, to find new values. (His frustrated search for them brings a Utopian strain into the novel.) Although Ulrich is embarrassed by such vague terms as 'soul,' he knows that man has a non-rational element; he seeks for a synthesis of 'precision and soul.' Until he finds it, he is without qualities, for the old ones are obsolete.

Thus Ulrich's 'problem' is a philosophical one, and helps to explain the proliferation of 'essayism' in the book. By this term Musil meant his excursuses on all sorts of subjects. While most of them are delightfully ironic, they bear down heavily on the narrative.

Der Mann ohne Eigenschaften has a very large cast of characters; many of them seem more realized than Ulrich himself or than his sister and spiritual twin Agathe. As in *Doktor Faustus*, we learn a great deal about the protagonist, but he is so extreme a biological 'sport' that it is difficult to visualize him. Some of the men Ulrich encounters are recognizable caricatures of actual persons: thus Arnheim is a devastating portrayal of Walter Rathenau, and Meingast probably represents the anti-rationalist 'philosopher' Ludwig Klages. In depicting the sex-murderer Moosbrugger, Musil used police records,[19] but the main reason for introducing him is to expose Ulrich to irrational evil in the guise of apparent harmlessness; the psychotic is quiet and pleasant except when his mania strikes him.

In the first (and most successful) part of the novel, Musil holds his plot together by using the device of the *Parallelaktion*. This 'collateral campaign' is a scheme to outshine the projected German celebration of Wilhelm II's thirtieth year as Kaiser in 1918, at which time Franz Joseph would have ruled Austria-Hungary for seventy years. Franz Joseph is to be hailed as 'the emperor of peace.' A further irony is less obvious: the planners of the demonstration are unable to agree on its theme. There is also a parallel between it and the disorganization which Ulrich finds among his friends.

Agathe is by far the person closest to Ulrich. The brother and sister feel that each of them is the 'other half' of the other. As in Mann's *Der Erwählte*, they justify their incest—which dominates the latter part of the novel—by their belief that no third person is worthy of either of them; they also believe that the ideal mystic individual must be androgynous. (There is explicit reference to the *Symposium* and to the myth of Isis and Osiris.) Yet their 'journey to Paradise' via symbolic incest fails. No one knows how Musil might have ended the enormous book or whether he could have done so.

Hermann Broch (1886–1951) has often been compared to Joyce and Proust. While his work does show a link to Joyce, it is actually closer to that of his fellow Viennese, Musil. Both spent much time in extraliterary spheres; neither was primarily an aesthete. Appropriately, both were interested in presenting and criticizing a culture as a whole, which involves them in 'essayism' or other digressive devices. They tend to write 'novels which are no longer novels.' A major difference between their *œuvres* is one of tone: Broch is ardent, Musil maintains an air of detachment.

At forty-one, Broch, a prominent businessman, enrolled as a student of mathematics, philosophy, and psychology at the University of Vienna. Four years later he surprised his friends by publishing his first novel. When Hitler took over Austria, Broch was imprisoned; on his release, he went to the United States, where he lived for a time at Princeton and later held an honorary post at Yale. Besides continuing to write and revise his literary work, he devoted himself to an ambitious study of mass psychology.

Basically, Broch's orientation was ethical and religious: a strong mystical strain appears in some of his narratives. His major themes are the decay of values and the decline of cultures, but he maintains a hope of renascence. Without a new 'world picture' this would be impossible; and since science cannot furnish an inclusive view of life, the novel must try to do so. Increasingly, Broch's novels reflect his sense of commitment. Often he succumbed to the danger of being too explicitly the preacher and philosopher in his fiction, but his voice, like that of one crying in the wilderness, demands respect.

Broch's first novel, the trilogy *Die Schlafwandler* (1931–32), is a symmetrically arranged triptych of a declining society. It ranges from naturalism to metaphysics, from fiction to passages of philosophical reflection, from fast-moving prose to verse. As German society becomes more hectic, the style changes accordingly. Thus the first volume, *1888. Pasenow oder die Romantik*, owes much to Fontane; the second, *1903. Esch oder die Anarchie*, is naturalistic; the third, *1918. Huguenau oder die Sachlichkeit*, is close to expressionism.

In *Pasenow*, the term romanticism in the title implies devotion to false values—the hero makes a cult of the Prussian code of military honour—and a corresponding neglect of true values. The protagonist abandons the warm-hearted Czech girl who loves him to make a dull marriage within his class.—Esch, in the second volume, is an uprooted petit bourgeois who strays into the 'anarchic' society of circus performers. He survives any number of wild adventures, but cannot reach his real goal, America. While not completely defeated, he attains only a certain rather drab stability.—In *Huguenau*, the impact of the war has destroyed the last remaining values; *Sachlichkeit* connotes the spurious objectivity of the amoralist. Utterly ruthless, the deserter Huguenau does not shrink at murder. He ends as a prosperous burgher, but will always be tortured by anxiety.

All three protagonists are somnambulists: Pasenow cannot awake to true values, Esch confuses freedom with anarchy, Huguenau is morally blind. The world of 1918 seems completely lost, the *Logos* is not perceived, false absolutes abound; but for these very reasons, Broch believes, a new age must soon dawn.

In a similar vein, *Die Schuldlosen* (1950; a novel composed of eleven episodes, some of them written twenty years earlier), argues that there is a link between personal selfishness and political decay. Broch's protagonist is a rich young man, Andreas. Like almost all of the other characters in the book, he is not evil; but he too shirks responsibility, not least in the area of politics. Like *Die Schlafwandler*, the book deals with three symmetrically placed years—in this case, 1913, 1923, 1933. As the last date hints, these 'innocents' have helped to smooth Hitler's path to power.

In a way reminiscent of Hofmannsthal's Claudio (in *Der Tor und der Tod*), Andreas never engages himself, never truly lives. He hurts people who love him, above all a young girl who takes her own life; for this he is severely punished. At the end, acknowledging that he is far from guiltless, Andreas commits suicide. Repeatedly the term *Seelenlärm* denotes the noisy, pseudo-soulful protestations of the insincere, but Andreas, again like Claudio, has attained an instant of authenticity in his death.

Deliberately plain and often harsh verses, entitled 'Stimmen,' at the beginning of each major division of the novel point out the moral and its political application. One line reads:

'Leb wohl Europa; die schöne Tradition ist zu Ende.'

Broch employs various symbols, primarily the triangle; this seems to evoke 'the artificially isolated existence that tries to shield itself from commitment. . . .'[20] Abundant allusions to the myth of *Don Juan*, especially to the 'Stone Guest,' serve to hold the book together; archetypal characters and leitmotifs suggest a debt to Thomas Mann.

Like *Doktor Faustus*, *Der Versucher** attempts to portray the rise of Nazism in symbolic form. An evil magician, Marius Ratti (*Rattenfänger*?) comes to an Austrian village, where he manages to fascinate most of the inhabitants.[20] Ratti is triumphant; but over against him stands the figure of Mutter Gisson (a nature goddess; her name is an anagram of gnosis). There are also hints that a village girl will give birth to a saviour. Alas, Broch's expressions of hope are less convincing than his statement of despair.

Der Tod des Vergil (1945) seems at first glance somewhat far from Broch's usual 'line,' but its theme is characteristic. For although this long 'inner monologue,' Broch's most Joycean book, is highly abstract and experimental, it deals basically with Broch's central problem: how can we move from a dying age into a new epoch? Everything is seen through the eyes of Vergil; the action, such as it is, is compressed into eighteen hours. The poet's desire to destroy the *Aeneid* reflects the sense of crisis in an apocalyptic age: dare one indulge in aesthetic activity at such a time? Few goals are more admirable than Broch's hope of reconciling literature and conscience.

---

* Broch never completed this work; he was working on a third version when he died, and the text published in 1953 consists of selections from all three manuscripts. Even the title is not Broch's own.

7 The Drama and Lyric After the First War*

"Man muss noch Chaos in sich haben, um einen tanzenden Stern gebären zu können."

—Nietzsche

"Things fall apart, the centre cannot hold."

—Yeats

During the years between 1918 and Hitler's rise to power, the literature of the Weimar Republic and of Austria was rich, varied, and indeed chaotic. Several of the established major figures—Rilke, Thomas Mann, Hesse, and Musil—reached new heights; some erstwhile expressionists, like Kaiser, Toller, Werfel, and above all Brecht, created challenging works in various modes. (Most of the great émigré writers, moreover, continued to be productive in exile.) Yet there were in fact no great unifying ideas, no 'vital centre,' either in literature or in politics. The few years of stability of the middle and late Twenties were preceded by revolution and inflation, and followed by depression and dictatorship.

Although it seemed impractical to discuss in this brief book poets like Oskar Loerke or Konrad Weiss, dramatists like Max Mell or Ferdinand Bruckner, or the satirist Kurt Tucholsky, their noninclusion implies no denial of their intrinsic interest.† Rather, it would appear more useful to limit my account to authors whose significance has been more firmly established. Similarly, although important essays by Rudolf Alexander Schröder and Rudolf Borchardt were published during this period—as well as by Hesse, Hofmannsthal, Heinrich and Thomas Mann, and others—it was not feasible to treat the essay or other relatively minor genres. Only in the case of that unique figure, Karl Kraus, has an exception been made.

---

* A few Nazi writers are listed in the following 'interchapter,' which also briefly considers the more significant emigrant writers of the second rank.

† For descriptions and evaluations of their work see the literary histories of Bithell, David, and Soergel-Hohoff.

From 1918 to 1933 Hauptmann was considered, in part because of the humane compassion of his early plays, *the* poet of the Weimar Republic. After that, the Nazis were astute enough to leave him in peace, even when he criticized them. When the Red Army invaded his native Silesia, the soldiers treated him with great respect.

Yet celebration as the unofficial laureate of the Republic was a dubious boon for him. As Hauptmann's production became more and more various, its lack of discipline increased. His head and profile resembled those of Goethe in old age, which led him to attempt the role of Wolfgang II. Not only did he try to rival Goethe in various genres and Dante in *terza rima*; he naïvely believed that in *Hamlet in Wittenberg* he had improved Shakespeare. Nevertheless, he did write, between 1918 and his death in 1946, several works which command respect.

The long novella* 'Der Ketzer von Soana' (1918) is often considered Hauptmann's finest prose work though its ardent sexuality is too overheated for some. Afraid of his own sensuality, a priest becomes a hermit in the Italian Alps, where he encounters an attractive, uninhibited peasant girl; as so often in German literature, Dionysos overcomes the 'pale Galilean.' The imagery is appropriately erotic.

Like all sensitive Europeans, at least those in the defeated nations, Hauptmann realized that the First World War had radically altered the shape of things. He was impelled to provide a symbolic account of this great change, as were Mann, Hofmannsthal, Musil, and Karl Kraus, among others. Curiously, he selected a renowned medieval rogue as the protagonist of his epic in dactylic hexameters, *Till Eulenspiegel* (1928), making him an ex-aviator to bring him up to date. In Hauptmann, Eulenspiegel's experiences are rather cosmic than comic. Although the scamp still plays tricks, his main experiences are seen as forming a cultural grand tour through the ages, during which he meets persons as different as Wagner's Amfortas, Johann Sebastian Bach, and Friedrich Ebert,† and undergoes

---

* Since Hauptmann's contribution to prose fiction was relatively slight at this time, it is convenient to treat the novella together with his works in other genres.

† First president of the Weimar Republic.

experiences ranging from a journey to ancient Greece to the murder of the Romanovs.

To illuminate Till's adventures Hauptmann uses here a bizarre myth of his own invention. God appears as 'Gott Barnum*-Saturn.' He thought this his greatest work, but one cannot produce a valid picture of an age without possessing taste and intellectual insight; *Eulenspiegel* cannot bear comparison with *Der Zauberberg*, *Der Turm*, or the major novels of Musil and Broch.

In *Der grosse Turm*, another long poem, Hauptmann belatedly atoned for his support of Hitler's regime in 1933. Tercets like the following are hardly poetry but reveal great courage:

> Den Thron Europas nimmt er ein, geschwollen
> von Gift. Er speist mit einem blutigen Latz
> ein Hundragout: von Hunden, doch von tollen.

Presumably he escaped punishment because by the time of publication (1942), the Nazis were too self-confident to care about the sentiments of an eighty-year-old poet.

A few of Hauptmann's late dramas deserve mention. *Dorothea Angermann*, another of his tragedies of seduction, returns to the naturalistic mood. Largely autobiographical, *Vor Sonnenuntergang* (1932) was obviously intended to round off his production as a counterpart to his first play *Vor Sonnenaufgang*. It is appropriately elegiac.

Yet his sun was not ready to set: the *Atriden-Tetralogie*† is one of Hauptmann's major dramatic achievements since the days of the Freie Bühne. His approach is characteristically pessimistic: he has no faith in the Olympian gods, but acknowledges the power of dark, chthonic forces. Men are mere puppets of fate; thus moral guilt does not exist—Hauptmann seems never to have abandoned the determinism of his youth. At the end, Orest is freed of guilt, but Iphigenie kills herself, thus fulfilling the sacrifice attempted at Aulis.—Unfortunately, the very conventional, 'epigonic' blank verse gravely weakens this potentially impressive work. Of course the writer's métier is language; and one may doubt that works

* The famous organizer of circuses.

† *Iphigenie in Delphi*, 1941; *Iphigenie in Aulis*, 1944; *Agamemnons Tod* and *Elektra*, 1948.

without distinction or freshness of style will long endure, except as social documents.[1]

Hofmannsthal's *Der Schwierige* (1921) is the finest of the few comedies of manners in German. Indeed, a reflection of the Austrian aristocracy, it confirms George Meredith's belief that high comedy can flourish only in the sophisticated society of a great city. Writing in a time of disastrous defeat, Hofmannsthal expressed his confidence in the old values of Austrian society. The *nouveaux*, like the hero's new servant or the Prussian *Neu*hoff, are brash and conceited, whereas the admirable heroine is named Helene *Alten*wyl.

Count Hans Karl Bühl, the *Schwieriger* from whom the play takes its name, is, except for Helene, the least difficult, most accessible of its characters: most of the others admire him, and several seek his advice. He gives sagacious advice to others but finds it extremely difficult to reach decisions about his own affairs. Highly sensitive, excessively modest, he has been well compared to Lessing's Tellheim (in *Minna von Barnhelm*).[2] Further, he is oppressed by the difficulty of communication, reminiscent in a less bitter way of the 'Chandos Letter.'* Like Hofmannsthal, Hans Karl was to discover that whereas words alone cannot suffice, the difficulty of communication can be surmounted. He is also far stronger than he and some others realize; his dismissal of the impertinent servant is a case in point. The play suggests that tact and moderation may very well go with strength. Apparently Hofmannsthal felt this synthesis particularly Austrian: the North German Neuhoff is energetic but personally impossible—like several other *Reichsdeutsche* in Austrian literature.

Baroness Helene, long in love with Bühl, embodies an ideal: she is gracious, tactful, but utterly resolute in a crisis. Much younger than he, she yet has clearer insight into essentials. When Bühl, recalling a moment of danger in the war when he thought of her as his wife, unconsciously declares his love, she draws the consequences. After embarrassing hesitations between 'Du' and 'Sie,' she takes the initiative at whatever risk of compromising herself, and overcomes his *Schwierigkeit*. The comedy ends on a universal note: the issues are not merely Austrian but human. While it occasions no raucous laughs, it has a Mozartian serenity; one can see or read it repeatedly.

* See pp. 26; 29.

Hofmannsthal's last, most ambitious work is the tragedy *Der Turm* (two versions, 1925; 1927). Although not a completely realized aesthetic unit like *Der Schwierige*, it is moving and impressive, especially in its second version, with its prophecy of the coming tyranny of evil. The poet laboured over it for years, in the attempt to make it sufficiently theatrical.

Appropriately, Hofmannsthal set his dark fable in 'a century like the seventeenth in atmosphere,' the era of the Thirty Years War. His main source was Calderón's *Life is a Dream*, but he drew on Grimmelshausen for the brutal atmosphere of the time and for his villainous Olivier, besides borrowing widely from the Bible, Shakespeare, and elsewhere. In general there is an embarrassment of riches, an overabundance of reference which is appropriately baroque but still overwhelming. Thus the charismatic hero, Sigismund, represents both the 'true king' and the poet;[3] in the second version he becomes rather the Christlike martyr than the tragic protagonist. Most of Hofmannsthal's favourite themes appear: the persistence of the past, the unlived life, responsibility, the threat of anarchy to tradition.[4] Each important character is simultaneously an individual, a social type, and a metaphysical symbol.

The basic fable however is simple. The king's son Sigismund, whom his father fears because of an oracle, is brought up in a filthy hovel like a beast. Yet he represents what Kafka called 'the indestructible in man'; once freed from the hovel, he seems irresistible: he overthrows his evil father and will apparently inaugurate a better order. Assassinated by the brutal Olivier, he gives place to the Children's King, who similarly represents incorruptibility. Sigismund's last words are: 'Bear witness: I was there. Even if no one knew me.'—In the second version the Children's King does not appear: when the Christlike Sigismund is killed, evil is completely victorious.

Having lost faith in the possibility of a synthesis of power and spirit, Hofmannsthal seems to have come to believe that evil will always defeat *Geist* in this world. The tragedy has a strongly Catholic tone; in the latter version this darkens to a radically pessimistic, 'baroque' religious attitude. At his request Hofmannsthal was buried in a monk's garments;[5] perhaps, like Werfel, he was inwardly converted to Christianity but did not wish to take any formal or public steps. With seismographic sensitivity, Hofmannsthal surmised that a catastrophe was coming—if not the decline of the West, something very close to it. His Olivier is a Hitlerian figure.

Probably *Der Turm* is too abstract, as well as too complicated, for stage success. Lines like Sigismund's 'Eitel ist alles ausser der Rede zwischen Geist und Geist,' have an austere beauty but are hardly dramatic. Yet since his death in 1929 Hofmannsthal's reputation has risen steadily, while that of many writers once more highly esteemed has fallen. Claude David has put the reasons for this shift excellently:

> . . . he defends a culture, he remains true to an art of moderation in an immoderate, violent epoch. As the troubles [of that epoch] recede into the distance of history, his quiet light shines more and more brightly.[6]

Bertolt Brecht's greatest success during the years of the Weimar Republic was the *Dreigroschenoper* (1928; music by Kurt Weill). While it may seem paradoxical that his Marxist equation of criminality with success in business should be enormously popular with bourgeois audiences, the reasons are not obscure. Basically, the work is too amusing to be taken seriously; the shock effect of the action and some of the lyrics amounts only to titillation; the audience is amused, not moved. In other words, the work is 'culinary,' a luxury article not a call to arms.

Brecht's *Die Heilige Johanna der Schlachthöfe* is closer to the political party 'line.' Here Joan Dark, a Salvation Army girl who works in his mythic Chicago, is converted to communism and comes to the conclusion that anyone who believes in God or other bourgeois illusions should be liquidated. Bitter parodies of Goethe and Schiller harmonize with the general mood of the piece.

The extremely bare, didactic plays of the late Twenties and the Thirties seem considerably less interesting. Somehow, however, Brecht became a great dramatist during his years in exile: his fame rests most securely on four, or possibly five dramas completed then (some were extensively revised later) or in the postwar period.*

In the lyric, Brecht reveals heights and depths, moments of genuine poetry and crude propaganda, much as he does in his dramas. In early ballads like "Vom armen B.B." and "Vom ertrunkenen Mädchen" there is a combination of passion and wit

* See below, pp. 135–138.

reminiscent of his master Villon; yet he can be extremely bare. Some of his serious verses are very powerful, like his apostrophe to his native country in 1933:

O Deutschland, bleiche Mutter!

or his question in "An die Nachgeborenen":

Aber wie kann ich essen und trinken, wenn
Ich dem Hungerndern entreisse, was ich esse. . . ?

On the other hand, many of his verses, like "Die Erziehung der Hirse" with its glorification of Stalin and Lysenko, are barely readable today. Brecht's unevenness is almost as striking as his range.

Although Carl Zuckmayer (b. 1896) is one of the most productive contemporary playwrights—he has also published lyrics and prose narratives—his fame is primarily based on two comedies, *Der fröhliche Weinberg* (1925) and *Der Hauptmann von Köpenick* (1931). In both, Zuckmayer, the son of a Roman Catholic wine-dealer, subjects the Prusso-German establishment to sharp but basically good-humoured satire.

After unsuccessful efforts to become an *avant-garde* writer, Zuckmayer scored his first great 'hit' with *Der fröhliche Weinberg*. Written partly in dialect and set in his native Rhineland, this very earthy comedy deals with the Aristophanic themes of wine and sex: only a man who has demonstrated his virility before marriage may marry the daughter of the rich vintner. After a night of drinking and love-making, the young hero, predictably, wins the hand of the heiress; other amorous couples are also involved in the action. The play owed its popularity not only to its broad, lusty humour but to the sense that it brought the drama down to earth—in every sense—after the hectic flights of expressionism. From this time on, Zuckmayer tended to a moderate conservatism in style.

While *Der fröhliche Weinberg* deals satirically with only one major character, a conceited 'corps student,' *Der Hauptmann von Köpenick* is concerned with the military and social system which obtained under the Hohenzollerns. Zuckmayer uses an actual historical incident: a poor outsider had enjoyed a brief period of glory; by pretending to be an officer he had exploited the German weakness for uniforms and titles. (To stress that he was not writing a documentary drama, Zuckmayer subtitled the play 'a German fairy tale.') The tone is more genial than that of Hauptmann's very comparable comedy *Der Biberpelz*, and the play abounds in good humour and typically impudent Berlin wit. Perhaps this makes its indictment of militarism all the more devastating.

When the Nazis come to power, Zuckmayer emigrated to Austria and eventually to the United States, where he continued to write but supported himself by farming in Vermont. When he returned to Germany shortly after the war, he had finished the most convincing of his serious dramas, *Des Teufels General* (1946).

Here Zuckmayer considered a theme suggested by the career of a personal friend, a famous aviator who became a general in the *Luftwaffe*. A charming and warm person, the flier fights for 'the devil' because of boyish naïveté and misguided patriotism. Upon realizing the true situation, he attempts to protect members of the German resistance. Finally, he kills himself by crashing an experimental aeroplane.

Like *Des Teufels General*, *Der Gesang im Feuerofen* (1950) and *Das kalte Licht* (1955) centre on questions of loyalty and betrayal. The first deals with the fate of a group of members of the French resistance—and of a young German soldier who joined them—the second, suggested by the defection of Klaus Fuchs, with the secrets surrounding the atom bomb, and the moral struggles of a man who gave them away. In both, Zuckmayer is on the side of the angels, but in both he descends to triteness and wordy editorializing. His strength lies in humour, emotion, and a sense of milieu, not in the analysis of moral or intellectual problems. Precisely because *Des Teufels General* presents persons of a sort he knew well, it is by far the most convincing of his later plays.

Rilke's most striking achievement is the *Duineser Elegien*, and their inception and composition were appropriately spectacular. Walking one stormy day in 1912 along the sheer walls of Castle Duino, 200 feet above the sea, he seemed to hear a voice cry from the wind:

> Wer, wenn ich schriee, hörte mich denn aus der Engel
> Ordnungen?

These are the opening words of the First Elegy. The second and Third were completed before the war, and some others begun. Then a long period of frustration set in, until in February, 1922, an even greater breakthrough occurred, in the Chateau de Muzot in Switzerland, where Rilke had isolated himself. A triumphant telegram to a friend reads: 'Seven Elegies now generally ready . . . Joy and wonder.' Two days later he finished the Tenth; in the same month he wrote the fifty-five *Sonette an Orpheus* and certain related poems. It was perhaps the greatest burst of creativity in modern literature: Rilke was 'possessed' by forces and images welling up from the unconscious.

These ten magnificent Elegies are written in irregular, unrhymed lines, mainly long, with many dactyls. As in Hölderlin's later poetry, the images and diction are bold and stark, but not bizarre. The Elegies are difficult but no more so than the finest of T. S. Eliot's work: they equally reward the careful reader. Rilke still displays his virtuosity of language on occasion, as in the Fifth:

> . . . er wringt sie,
> biegt sie, schlingt sie und schwingt sie,
> wirft sie und fängt sie zurück.

These lines are typical in drawing an unexpected parallel between the metaphysical and the ordinary: here the effects of the will on human beings are equated with the jugglings of acrobats.

Broadly speaking, the great themes of the *Elegien* are human loneliness; perfection (in the angels) over against humanity; life and death, regarded as two halves of a *Doppelbereich*; love and lovers; the hero; true existence versus mere duration; the task of the poet; lamentation and praise.

The angels, creatures of inhuman perfection, have nothing to do with Christianity; they bring no messages to man. In their beauty and especially as representatives of poetic inspiration, they are unbearable to humans—'fast tödliche Vögel der Seele.' They are magnificent, timeless, and changeless. While they have been compared to Hölderlin's gods,[7] Günther's statement that their basic meaning is artistic is more helpful.[8] Yet men, inferior in a sense even to animals, can perform one task the angels cannot: as the 'bees of the invisible' they transform experience into works of art. Performing the aesthetic miracle, man changes things into symbols and images of the inner sphere—*Weltinneraum*.

Stating briefly the major themes of the individual Elegies should give some notion of the architecture of the whole cycle. The First deals with the loneliness and evanescence of existence—'Denn Bleiben ist nirgends.' Other themes are: the poet, lovers, the young dead, the acceptance of death. More focused, the Second contrasts angels to man, who has lost what authenticity he had. In the Third, Rilke sets the blind sexual passion of man—'jenen verborgenen schuldigen Fluss-Gott des Bluts'—against the love of woman. The next two are very dark: the Fourth states man's inferiority to puppets, and the Fifth takes a group of acrobats as symbols of our shabbiness and clumsiness; elsewhere, perhaps, grace is achieved. Striking a firmer note, the Sixth celebrates the hero and his death; death is to life as the fruit to the flower. The Seventh is a hymn of praise: 'Hiersein ist herrlich,' and develops man's role as the transmuter of the visible to the invisible. Then lament is reasserted, in the Eighth: we cannot achieve pure existence—'das Nirgends ohne Nicht'—but must experience life dualistically, splitting subject from object. The Ninth develops this idea further: only when *vis-à-vis* tangible things can we perform the labour of transformation. (Thus man's glory flows directly, inevitably, from his misery.) Finally, the Tenth has as its main subject sorrow and its affirmation. The *Leid-Stadt*, comparable to Eliot's 'Waste Land,' is the surrounding country, where one may meet personifications of lamentation, 'die Klagen.'

Naturally one should not turn to the *Elegien* for an articulated philosophy or Weltanschauung, and interpreters who persist in asking such inept questions receive strange answers. One does find there, along with poetry unsurpassed in our time, the insights of one of the most sensitive of men about the nature of human life. Here also is a radical expression of Rilke's belief that only aesthetic activity justifies human existence.

Products of the *annus mirabilis*, 1922, the *Sonette an Orpheus* are another of Rilke's great achievements.* To the generally mournful tone of the *Elegien* they oppose the theme of praise, of wholehearted acceptance of life. The change in mood is so marked that critics have used the term *Umschlag* (complete dialectical reversal) to describe it.

Manipulating the fourteen-line pattern of the sonnet with utmost skill, Rilke yet preserved his freedom. He varies greatly the length

* Like the *Elegien*, they were published in 1923.

of line, especially in the second part of the cycle, and replaces the traditional balance of octet against sestet by using the more flexible scheme: $4+4+3+3$. In intellectual terms, paradox is his major device; such apparent contradictions as 'Aber die Kinder . . ./ schreien an wirklichen Schreien vorbei' are common. The most memorable instance occurs in the last lines of the cycle:

> zu der stillen Erde sag: Ich rinne.
> Zu dem raschen Wasser sprich: Ich bin.

The Orpheus of the title *is* all song and poetry, one sonnet tells us; he is also the poet of course, and thus the god of Rilke's aesthetic universe.

Besides 'praise,' the great motifs of these sonnets include the affirmation of this world, the stress on transformation (*Wandlung, Verwandlung*), of relatedness (*Bezug*) as a unifying force, and of course poetry and the poet. Although most of the *Sonette* are very successful, the cycle does not quite rank, as a whole, with the *Elegien*. A few sonnets are marred by coyness, and the line about hunting—

> Töten ist eine gestalt unseres wandernden Trauerns . . .

is at best pseudo-profound.

After the *Sonetten* Rilke wrote a number of beautiful poems, but no long cycles. (See his posthumous *Späte Gedichte*, 1934.) He even ventured to compose in French, while living in French Switzerland, saying that a voice rose in him, and then the poems were there.[9] Unlike most poetic experiments in a foreign idiom, Rilke's are highly successful.

Rilke's fame as one of the few great poets of the twentieth century is secure. The danger of his work is its excessive stress on inwardness, with its consequent underrating of responsible action. Yet at the worst, this can harm only those who take his poems as guides to life.

The fame of Karl Kraus (1874–1936) rests mainly on his satiric talents, but he was also a gifted critic of language, an interpreter—in many successful public readings—of Shakespeare, Nestroy, Wedekind, and others, and a lyric poet of remarkable delicacy. Above all, he was a writer of great courage, quite ready to be called a revolutionary, a reactionary, or an unpatriotic scribbler as long as he had his say.

Kraus exerted influence on Austrian intellectual life primarily through his journal *Die Fackel* (1899–1936), to which he was the main contributor from the first, and after 1911 the only one. Witty and outspokenly polemical, *Die Fackel* carried on guerrilla warfare against the Viennese establishment and against the many manifestations of Austrian and German civilization Kraus disapproved of. (A somewhat comparable figure in American letters is H. L. Mencken, but one feels that Kraus was more fiercely in earnest and intellectually more serious.) Not interested in party politics, he was convinced that Austria was doomed: catastrophe was inevitable.

Paradoxically, one great target of Kraus's attack was journalism as such. Hypersensitive to vulgarity of thought and style, he believed that the press was ruining morals as well as letters. However exaggerated, his belief was no pose: when the newspaper *Neue Freie Presse* offered to put him in charge of its literary section, which would have made him the most powerful critic in Austria, he refused.

Kraus's bitter condemnation of Heine is part of his rejection of journalism, for he felt, and argued in *Heine und die Folgen* (1910), largely ignoring the last great poems, that the poet had dragged literature down to the level of the *feuilleton* and that he was an inferior human being. Although he was a man of great aesthetic sensitivity, Kraus consistently put morals first, maintaining that a man without character could not be a genius. With complete devotion to his own aspect of truth, and realizing that similar charges had been raised by anti-Semites and philistines, he followed his own convictions at whatever cost.

While Kraus appears eccentric indeed here, his monster drama of the First World War *Die letzten Tage der Menschheit* (1918–22) shows him in a better light. He was one of the few European intellectuals not swept away by patriotic excitement. Rather, the war confirmed his belief that the contemporary world would perish; reality turned out to be worse than his direst fears. In this enormously long play, which as Kraus said would fill some ten evenings, he constructed a great *montage* of Austrian and German life, on the fronts and behind them. Both Kaisers play a part, as do generals, profiteers, professors, journalists, preachers, even poets. Many contemporaries —including Hofmannsthal—appear under their own names; there are also many anonymous characters. The most damning and depressing aspect of the work is that Kraus quotes actual newspaper accounts, sermons, chauvinistic verses, etc. Since every class is corrupt, we come to feel that the last days of humanity have indeed come; men are changing into two-legged hyenas.—The author, cast as the *Nörgler* (fault-finder) frequently comments on the course of events.

With its over 200 scenes, the frequently repetitious work is indeed too long, even as a closet drama, yet its impact is great. In the last line God utters the famous words allegedly spoken by the Austrian emperor after the outbreak of war: 'Ich habe es nicht gewollt!'— which leaves the impression that the cosmos as a whole is as badly off as is Central Europe. Hell is victorious.

Believing that the decay of the *logos* is an infallible sign of corruption, Kraus held that no amount of attention to syntax, diction, or punctuation could be excessive. He boasted that he devoted maximum care to every sentence; he wrote essays about fine points of German usage; and once he successfully went to law against a person who had omitted a comma in reprinting one of his poems.[10] Kraus's own lyrics are melodious, surprisingly traditional in form, and often unexpectedly gentle in tone.

An alert and versatile critic, Kraus published several volumes of essays in addition to *Heine und die Folgen. Untergang der Welt durch schwarze Magie* and *Literature und Lüge* are probably the best known; Kraus ranges over many topics: literature of the past and present, the theatre, journalism of course, language, a law suit, moral questions, and the decadence of the contemporary world. There are some personal tributes and more polemics. Among his favourite targets was the once famous publicist Maximilian Harden; Kraus devoted several essays to 'translating' Harden's affected jargon into good prose. His hatred of psychoanalysis inspired the often-quoted epigram: 'Psychoanalysis is the disease of which it claims to be the cure.' Like many satirists, he became fiercely personal on occasion. At times he was downright cruel, writing for example of Hofmannsthal, when that poet's lyric vein had been exhausted, that he 'drank from golden goblets from which the wine has long since vanished.'

Renowned—and feared—for his wit, Kraus published three volumes of aphorisms. The title of the first—*Sprüche und Wider-*

9

sprüche—is typical of his way of making a 'mere' pun reveal some aspect of the truth neatly and economically: in this case, his 'nay-saying' attitude towards many of the mores and beliefs of his time. Like Novalis and Friedrich Schlegel, he believed in the mystic virtues of 'the word':[11] a play on words may guide the writer to a new insight; 'filing' one's style may, as Kraus put it, strike a spark. To Kraus, language itself has heuristic functions as well as creative ones. Thus he wrote that the term 'family bonds (*Familienbände*)' had the savour of truth in it; and—untranslatably—expressed the evanescence of life: 'Man lebt nicht einmal einmal.' (Hofmannsthal beautifully expressed this typically Viennese notion, but Kraus's formulation is sharper, perhaps more memorable.) As Liegler puts it, Kraus aimed at a 'dagger stab,' a quick devastating thrust.[12] His best epigrams rank with the sharpest of La Rochefoucauld and Lichtenberg.

Similarly, Kraus believed that rhyme was no mere ornament: there is an intrinsic relation between sound and sense.

> Der Reim ist nur der Sprache Gunst,
> nicht nebenher noch eine Kunst.

> Geboren wird er, wo sein Platz,
> Aus einem Satz mit einem Satz. . . .

> Es ist das Ufer, wo sie landen,
> Sind zwei Gedanken einverstanden. . . .

The pun on *Satz* (both 'sentence' and leap') is highly characteristic of Kraus.

The last years of Karl Kraus are those of the decline of the first Austrian republic. While he had no illusions about the Dollfuss regime, which he described as 'fascism tempered by sloppiness (*Schlamperei*),' he supported it as a lesser evil than Nazism, finding that movement beneath satiric attack. Sensing that an epoch was ending, he closed his last poem with the line:

> Das Wort entschlief, als jene Welt erwachte.

Interchapter: The Nightmare, 1933-1945

"... *Elend*, n. ahd. *elilenti*
... 'Ausland, Verbannung, Not'."
—Kluge-Götze, *Etymologisches Wörterbuch*

1. The Emigration

Hitler's accession to power caused the greatest exodus of gifted persons in modern times. Of the major writers, only Benn and the senescent Hauptmann stayed in Germany; the Manns, Brecht, and George left, and Musil voluntarily emigrated from Austria in 1938.

Of course, the Jews suffered far more than any other group. While most of the other *émigrés* were forced to leave for political reasons, a surprisingly large number departed of their own volition —a fact supporting Burke's statement that one cannot indict a nation. In this case, to be sure, one must indict a disturbingly large fraction of contemporary Germans and Austrians. Among the other voluntary exiles were Kaiser, Karl Barth, Leonhard Frank, and H. H. Jahnn. Men of all parties left—including even a few former members of the Nazi party who became disgusted or at least frightened.

The story is a harrowing one: many of the exiles went through excruciating trials. Suicide was frequent: among the more noted writers Hasenclever, Toller, and Stefan Zweig took their lives; there were many others. A number emigrated rather than divorcing their Jewish wives. While many others escaped at the last moment, the experience must have left indelible scars. Heinrich Mann had to walk over the Pyrenees when he was almost seventy; Freud was in grave personal danger but was ransomed at the last moment. For a multitude of others, no refuge was found.

Perhaps the greatest injury to the writers *as writers* was the alienation from their own language. Not only did all but the most famous lose their publics; separation from countries where their language was alive was far more serious. Deprived of their medium, most of the exiled authors faced the problem of making bricks without straw. Many of them went first to cities where the German language was spoken by all, as in Vienna; or by a sizeable minority, as in Prague; or at least to such literary centres as Paris; after a few years, they were faced, at best, by renewed flight. A few learned to write in a new language, but most were forced to support themselves in a different field. Some of the relatively fortunate obtained academic positions. It is all the more remarkable that admirable works were written: not only by masters like the Manns and Brecht.* Anna Seghers, for example, wrote her finest novel, *Das siebte Kreuz*, in exile.

Besides authors already named in this context, a long line of well-known writers should be mentioned. It included Broch, Döblin, Bruno Frank, Ödön von Horváth, Theodor Plievier, Ludwig Renn, Joseph Roth, René Schickele, Franz Werfel, Karl Wolfskehl, Arnold Zweig and hundreds of lesser figures. Of course, there were scholars deeply concerned with literature, like Ernst Cassirer and Erich Auerbach, as well as painters, sculptors, and musicians. There were in fact men and women of every profession and of most of the other occupations. Aside from temporary refuges like Austria and Czechoslovakia, the main asylums were the United States, Britain, Turkey, and Palestine; Soviet Russia admitted few of the exiles after 1938. Both the culture and the power of the nations relatively generous to the fugitives were strikingly increased; Germany and Austria were correspondingly weakened. Retribution was not long delayed.

2. *Literature within Germany*

> ". . . Wort wurde trockenes Etwas und es war als sei
> Verständigung uns für immer genommen.
> Wer noch dichtete war ein verächtlicher Narr,
> der aus Früchten welke Blumen erzeugt."
>
> —*Hermann Broch*

---

* For discussions of works written in exile by the major figures, see Chaps. 6 and 8.

While Thomas Mann's remark of 1945 that all books published in Germany under Hitler's rule should be pulped sprang from an only too justifiable disgust, it goes much too far—aside from the point that destroying books should be left to the totalitarians. After all, the first two volumes of his own *Joseph* were published in Nazi Germany; Jewish writers were allowed to publish in 'segregated' presses until 1938 as long as their 'racial' origin was clearly indicated; some religious leaders and theologians, Protestant and Catholic, showed great courage, and several scholars—though relatively few —argued bravely against this or that Nazi dogma. Furthermore, certain tolerated writers, mainly conservative nationalists, Christians, or both, developed great skill in subtly implying resistance to the regime. The flight into the historical novel,[1] like Kästner's concentration on children's books, was a way of 'distancing' oneself from the Nazis. It was the poets who most often raised their voices in protest. Perhaps their employment of symbolic 'veiling' imagery afforded them a degree of freedom; perhaps it was the Nazi scorn of any lyric not 'rooted in the soil,' or 'in the folk.' Yet as the dictatorship became more absolute, things approached the state described in the lines quoted at the beginning of this section. 1935 was worse than 1933; 1939 far worse than 1935. Some authors stopped publishing; some, like Barlach and Benn, were forbidden even to submit manuscripts, on pain of the concentration camp.

Among the genuine 'inner emigrants' were Hans Carossa and— rather surprisingly—Ernst Jünger, who refused membership in the Nazified Prussian *Dichterakademie*, and Ricarda Huch, who resigned from it. Jünger's brother, Friedrich Georg, included the poem 'Der Mohn' in his *Gedichte* (1934; Berlin); it contains such unmistakable references to National Socialism as 'das kindische Lied ruhmloser Trunkenheit.' Presumably the well-known conservative tendency of Jünger and the nationalist stance of his publisher Ernst Niekisch disarmed the censor. Jünger was not imprisoned, but after the appearance of this volume he was threatened and otherwise harassed by the Gestapo. Even as late as 1939 Ernst Jünger was able to publish *Auf den Marmorklippen*, an allegorical novel which condemns totalitarianism unambiguously. It seems highly probable that the regime found it impolitic to punish Jünger, a war hero and an author highly esteemed by the German Right, when the government was launching another war. A considerable number of other conservative writers managed to stand aside, maintaining their dignity, and yet to continue to publish. To some extent Roman Catholic authors may have been protected by their church, though one of the most gifted, Elisabeth Langgässer, was forbidden further publication in 1936. Gertrud von Le Fort, Werner Bergengruen, and Reinhold Schneider all played honourable if modest literary parts, as did the Protestant Ina Seidel and the non-Christian Ernst Wiechert. Once vastly overrated as a novelist, Wiechert wrote an account of his imprisonment in a concentration camp—*Der Totenwald* (1945), which is very powerful. Essayists like Rudolph Alexander Schröder* and the scholar Ernst Robert Curtius maintained their independence. Some of these writers were very nationalistic, some were admirers of the Prussian military tradition, but none of them condoned torture or murder.

On the whole the Rightist opposition was as brave (and as ineffectual, at least from the short-run point of view) as that offered by the Left and by certain religious groups. Communist, socialist, and liberal writers, like Jewish authors of any persuasion, could of course publish only outside occupied Europe. Yet their books did something to preserve, however diminished, the image of the 'other Germany.' Although their protest was necessarily muted and indirect, the writers who criticized the regime from within contributed to the same aim. Some even managed to find a public though not a publisher. Thus Rudolf Hagelstange, whose sonnet-cycle *Venezianisches Credo* was surreptitiously printed in Verona and appeared on Hitler's birthday (!), April 20, 1945,[2] played his part in somewhat mitigating the national disgrace. Even such apparently apolitical poems as those of Hermann Kasack make their point through a pervasive melancholy of diction and tone: 'Sybillinische Klagen,' published in *Das ewige Dasein* (1943) is a striking example.

It must, however, be stressed that 'inner emigration'† is far different from resistance. In the—politically ruinous—German tradition of inwardness, the 'inner emigrants' refrained from overt

* Schröder's close friend, the essayist, translator, and minor poet Rudolf Borchardt, had long been living in Italy.

† So many writers, after 1945, falsely claimed to have belonged to the inner emigration that the term came into disrepute, but quite a few honestly 'emigrated.'

action. Of course such action would have been extremely dangerous and in many cases virtually impossible. Few writers in any country have the physique or psyche to be heroes. An author rash enough to try to publish an obviously anti-Nazi manuscript would find neither a publisher, a printer, nor a bookseller; more likely, he would be denounced and disappear into a concentration camp; and no word of his protest would have appeared. While a few brave men wrote and circulated illegal anti-Nazi pamphlets, these were normally printed in some neighbouring country and smuggled over the border at enormous risk.

Despite the apparent hopelessness of their lot, several poets, like Albrecht Haushofer, Dietrich Bonhoeffer, Richard Billinger, and Günther Weisenborn, actually wrote lyrics in Nazi prisons or—a far more difficult feat—in concentration camps.[3] Even some poems composed in the Warsaw ghetto escaped destruction. When one thinks of the vast difficulty of smuggling anything out of these dungeons, and of the punishments inflicted on anyone detected writing or passing on anti-Nazi material, it is amazing that any of these works have survived. Billinger's *Nachtwache*, written in a Gestapo prison in Munich, emphasizes resignation rather than protest. Nevertheless, its publication by S. Fischer in 1935 was a courageous gesture; it would have been impossible a few years later. After publishing three political dramas, which deal ostensibly with Roman themes but have implicit reference to the German dictatorship, Haushofer wrote his *Moabiter* Sonette* during his imprisonment of 1944-45. Published in 1946, these sonnets comprise his one famous book. They are traditional in style but are distinguished by rare ethical nobility. Haushofer had been arrested after the attempted revolt against Hitler collapsed on July 20, 1944; it was his second arrest by the Nazis. Two weeks before the war ended he was killed by the Gestapo.

3. *Nazi authors*

"Zu Hitler fällt mir gar nichts ein."—*Karl Kraus*

Only a very few writers, none of them of real eminence, were

* They take their name from the Berlin district Moabit, where the prison was located.

members of the Nazi party when it came to power in 1933—persons like Heinrich Anacker and Baldur von Schirach, who are memorable only historically at best. Many of the Nazis, from Hitler down, had artistic, literary, or philosophical ambitions. Peter Viereck[4] has shown that many of the leading Nazis were frustrated intellectuals, 'armed Bohemians.' Even Dr. Goebbels wrote a novel, *Michael*, which is no worse and no better than the average product of his party. This complete absence of literary distinction cannot be insignificant.

To be sure, two burnt-out expressionists, Hans Johst and Arnolt Bronnen, were strong sympathizers. Others flocked to Hitler's standard—Pan-Germanists, believers in salvation through 'blood and soil,' pseudo-philosophers like E. G. Kolbenheyer, and sheer opportunists. Of course, fascist writers were not a German monopoly by any means: there were Céline, Knut Hamsun, various Italians, Ezra Pound, and so on. The most notable fact about the German 'parlour fascists' was their lack of talent.

8 *Partial Recovery: German Literature After 1945**

Denn der Boden zeugt sie wieder,
Wie von je er sie erzeugt.
—*Faust*, 11, 9937f.

At the time of Germany's unconditional surrender in May, 1945, the nation was in a state of utter collapse. With a very few exceptions, the towns and the great cities lay in ruins; and the intellectual and moral destruction was even worse. The universities, degraded long before, had been closed since Goebbels' declaration of total war in 1943, and numerous churches, theatres, opera houses, and libraries had been destroyed or badly damaged. The roads were filled with refugees, Germans this time, with labourers from other countries whom the Nazis had forcibly pressed into their service, returning home, with Allied soldiers, prisoners of war, and men just released from concentration camps. To many, the problems of finding food and shelter seemed insoluble. Even worse was the mood of nihilism, despair, guilt, and self-pity. Aside from those war criminals who were brought to trial, the guilty, half-guilty, and innocent were faced with roughly the same stark situation.

Thus it is natural that German writers speak of this period as the 'zero point.' Grim though it was, there were certain alleviating factors—in literature, to which we must confine ourselves, as elsewhere. First of all, a surprising number of exiles returned: Brecht, Döblin, Plievier, Anna Seghers, Zuckmayer, and Arnold Zweig—to name a few of the more outstanding ones. Some, while not returning, re-established contact with German literary life, enlivening it even when they were the occasion of bitter polemics.

* In most cases, the discussion runs to about 1955, but I have set no rigid limit. Down to p. 138, the text is concerned with writers more or less established before 1945; then with the figures who did not emerge until after the war.

At least equally enlivening was the belated impact of other literatures. While the intellectual Chinese wall of the censorship had isolated the country for only twelve years, the Nazis had employed many other methods to discourage interest in any writers whom they considered cosmopolitan, liberal, pacifist, socialist, communist, Jewish, or in any sense *avant-garde*. Thus before 1945 only a handful of the younger generation was acquainted with the works of Joyce or Eliot. After the war, major influences came from France (existentialism; the experimental drama from Claudel to Beckett) and the United States (the novel, especially Hemingway's and Faulkner's, and the drama of O'Neill, Tennessee Williams, and Wilder). The 'land of poets and thinkers' had become a culturally underdeveloped nation; now the attempt to catch up proved exciting. In addition there was the discovery or rediscovery of writers in German whom the Nazis had banned or played down; Heine, Kafka, Benn, the Manns, and the expressionistic poets come to mind.

A few of the older authors who did not emigrate found sooner or later that their careers were stunted or completely blocked by Nazi persecution, the war, or both. For them the German defeat was indeed a liberation. To turn first to Gottfried Benn: mentioned above* as one of the leading expressionistic authors, Benn had a long, complex career. During the first part of his life, only the *avant-garde* esteemed him, but he emerged after 1945 as the most renowned lyric poet of the Federal Republic though possibly he was more praised than read, as Lessing said of Klopstock.

Formally, Benn's early poems and many of his later ones are expressionistic; in atmosphere and attitude, they are of a scepticism, often a cynicism which are at the opposite pole from the moral tone of Werfel, Stadler, Toller, and so on. Benn was a practising physician specializing in venereal diseases, and his earlier verses never let us forget the ugliness and horror of disease and dying. (See especially *Morgue* [1912,] his first volume of verse.) Influenced by the late works of Nietzsche, he scorned the man of the herd: he never joined in the celebration of man as such. Inevitably, he became a nihilist, who proclaimed that no values, including even the concept of individuality, still held. *Entfremdung* he thought was the word to describe relations between human beings.

* See pp. 64; 82f.

Benn's life was typical of the experiences of many intelligent but nationalistic Germans of his generation. In 1914, two years after his emergence as a poet, he became a military physician in occupied Brussels, but he managed to find time to continue his writing. After the war he settled in Berlin—the centre of everything experimental in the German arts—supported himself by his medical practice, and published his collected verse and prose, but wrote little. Yet he was admired greatly in liberal and leftist literary circles; he in turn publicly praised writers like Klabund and Heinrich Mann. In 1931, he stated in a lecture that collectivism was incompatible with poetry.*

Thus Benn's support of the 'Third Reich' in 1933 came as a nasty shock to many. He had, however, long been subject to anti-intellectual moods, expressed in lines like:

> O dass wir unsere Ururahnen wären.
> Ein Klümpchen Schleim in einem warmen Mohr.

When Klaus Mann, who had fled to France, protested, Benn affirmed his new-found faith in the *Volk* in his essay 'Der neue Staat und die Intellektuellen,' a triumph for Goebbels, who had Benn's avowal widely distributed.

Yet as Klaus Mann had prophesied, this strange alliance could not last. The Nazis discovered that Benn had written 'immoral' poems and banned all his work in 1937. For his part, Benn could not long dull his perceptions by so crude an opiate; he returned to the army, an act he typically called the 'aristocratic form of emigration.' Soon his disillusion turned to despairing hatred. In a poem of 1943, he wrote

> Die Pfütze prüft den Quell, der Wurm die Elle,
> die Kröte spritzt dem Veilchen in den Mund
> —Hallelujah!—

and envisioned the vultures gathering over Germany. Yet he served faithfully until the end; objectively he was helping Hitler.

In 1945 he returned to Berlin, resuming the practice of medicine

---

* See the excellent anthology, largely made up of translations of Benn, *Primal Vision* (Norfolk, Conn., n.d.), pp. 39–45.

under almost impossible conditions. Typically, it was a former emigrant who obtained Allied permission for Benn, deeply compromised though he was, to publish.[1] A spate of his books appeared in the years 1948–50; Benn became a national figure. In his case the *Schubladentheorie*—the largely mistaken notion that once Hitler fell, oppressed writers would take masterpieces from secret drawers—was vindicated.

Like Brecht, Benn often tried in his earlier verses deliberately to shock the reader. In technique he was indebted to Heine, Rilke (!), and probably George; thus a note of parody is often heard. Similarly, while the well-known poem 'D-Zug' apparently celebrates the 'griechisches Glück' which the returning vacationers have enjoyed by the Baltic, it actually demasks these lower middle-class Berliners by showing that their 'happiness' has consisted of the sheerest animality.

After Benn resumed publication in 1945—he had been banned by the Nazis but was regarded with suspicion by the Allied authorities—he wrote 'static' poetry* as he called it, calmer, less bitter, in a sense almost classic. These self-conscious verses make use of many scientific terms but are also rich in references to both classical and Christian myth. In the most successful poems the disparate elements are somehow transmuted into lyrics. Benn called himself an intellectualist, and has often been compared to T. S. Eliot, but he lacked Eliot's humanity as well as his Christianity. Above all, one suspects, he appealed because of his tone of utter disillusion. Like many of his countrymen in 1945, he believed that sheer survival was the only attainable goal, and a pragmatic approach the only sensible one.

Generally, the difficulty of Benn's poems is as great as the intelligence they reveal. (He wrote about 'atom-smashing' in 1937.) Since he did not believe in communication, it is only appropriate that his writings are often Delphic. Yet his belief that the poet should avoid 'mere feeling' and that the true artist, like reality, is cold, is a salutary counterweight to the romantic German tradition.

Belief in form as a value in itself saved the late Benn from complete nihilism, though it sounds like a sophisticated revival of—

---

* See the volume *Statische Gedichte*, 1948

faute de mieux—the aestheticism of the Nineties. Like the neo-romantics, he feels the 'changes of things':

> Leben ist Brückenschlagen
> über Ströme, die vergehn.

In a poem written the year before his death, Benn admits, amazingly, that an element of good exists after all:

> Ich habe mich oft gefragt und keine Antwort gefunden,
> woher das Sanfte und das Gute kommt,
> weiss es auch heute nicht und muss nun gehn.

Although the first works of Heimito von Doderer (b. 1896) were published in the Twenties, he did not emerge as a writer of importance until after the Second World War. His two most ambitious novels, *Die Strudlhofstiege* (1951) and *Die Dämonen* (1956) are long, rich, admirably plotted narratives about twentieth-century Vienna; they are baroque in richness of incident and luxuriance of language, but uneven in quality. When Doderer is good, he is very, very good. . . .

Die Strudlhofstiege is generally light in tone and concludes with the happy ending of a comedy. Its curious title comes from the handsome flight of stone steps connecting an aristocratic quarter of Vienna with the literally lower modest section inhabited by the lower middle class. Doderer focuses the novel on the development of Sektionsrat Melzer and the problematic intellectual René von Stangeler, who seems to be a projection of the author. Eventually both of them, modern analogues to Parsifal and Gawain, reach their goals. The *Strudlhofstiege* comes to stand for the centripetal forces of the Viennese tradition. Like *Tom Jones*, the book strikes one as a comedy in the form of a novel.

Of course the recent history of Austria has been far from comic, and *Die Dämonen*, which comes to grips with it, is far different in tone. The 'demons' are the forces which ruined the first Austrian republic, and the action culminates in the burning by rioters of the Palace of Justice in Vienna. Again there is an almost overwhelming variety of character and incident. The central symbol is the octopus, and the book's epigraph is appropriate: 'Malignitati falsa species libertatis inest'—'There is in ill-doing the false appearance of freedom.' (Tacitus).

Among the older writers who returned to literary life after the war was the conservative nationalist Ernst Jünger. His novel *Heliopolis* (1949) is a 'negative Utopia' like Kasack's *Die Stadt hinter dem Strom*: it presents a world of enormous technical perfection in which men behave as badly as ever. As in *Auf dem Marmorklippen* a conflict between a brutal tyrant and a cultivated élite dominates the scene. Quite clearly, *Heliopolis* is a metaphor of Germany in the late Thirties as it appeared to Jünger. In the novel the party of the 'Truly Noble' (*die Edeltrefflichen*), comprising the ruling prince, the army, and the protagonist (who recalls Jünger himself) oppose with varying success the rabble led by the sinister *Landvogt*;* the hero manages to save two members of a persecuted racial minority.

As always, Jünger's figures are symbolic types, not individuals. In recent years he has belatedly emancipated himself from the influence of Spengler and Nietzsche; he has come to place the humanistic ideal before the 'heroic' one.† Yet his novels, like such recent books of reminiscences as his *Gärten und Strassen* (1942) and *Strahlungen* (1949), still reveal a chilling lack of human sympathy. The attraction of his books lies in their imagery, their lucid and lucent style.

Hermann Kasack's *Die Stadt hinter dem Strom* (1947) is often called surrealistic; in this case, the fashionable label is quite correct. Simultaneously nightmarish and real, the novel betrays a large debt to Kafka. The protagonist visits a mysterious ruined city across a great river and learns that he is to become its archivist. To his delight, he meets there a woman he has long loved, but when they embrace, he realizes with horror that she is dead. Eventually he recrosses the river; he can never forget what he has seen and tries to tell others about it, but no one pays any attention. Written in large part during the bombings of 1942–44, the book presents not so much a city of the dead as an image of existence during and immediately after the war—a state closer to death than to life.

A former expressionist, Kasack was isolated throughout the Nazi

---

* It is hardly accidental that this title recalls the villain of Schiller's *Wilhelm Tell*.

† See p. 102.

régime but was allowed to make his living and to publish. Others, like Elisabeth Langgässer, were less fortunate. When the German government forbade Frau Langgässer any further publication, in 1936, it appeared that her promising career had been completely blighted. Yet she survived persecution (she was half-Jewish), the bombing of Berlin, poor health, and forced labour. In 1946 she published one of the most remarkable German novels of recent years, *Das unauslöschliche Siegel*.

Elisabeth Langgässer had established a solid if unspectacular reputation in the Twenties and early Thirties with novellas, a few radio plays, volumes of religious poetry, and the mythical novel *Proserpina*; *Das unauslöschliche Siegel* made her famous. It is religious, indeed frankly supernaturalistic in tone, and highly experimental in form. (Hermann Broch remarked that it was perhaps the first genuinely distinguished surrealistic novel.) With little interest in plot or traditional motivation, Frau Langgässer presented here a cosmic duel between God and Satan for the soul of Lazarus Belfontaine, a Jew whose baptism, once he has been truly converted, becomes an actually indelible seal. As in the Bible, Lazarus is reborn.

A net of symbols, images, and allusions helps to shape the meaning of this long, complex, and to some readers confusing book. Animal images emphasize the sinful element in man, water imagery the theme of death and rebirth.[2] Believing that a fleshly life leads directly to self-destruction, Frau Langgässer did not shrink from showing evil at its most drastic; the good prevails but only after dreadful struggles.—Similarly religious in orientation, the novel *Märkische Argonautenfahrt* (1950) shows, against the background of the German collapse, the pilgrimage of seven sinners in search of redemption.

During the second war Bertolt Brecht wrote, besides lesser works, three major plays: *Mutter Courage und ihre Kinder* (1941),* *Der gute Mensch von Sezuan* (1943), *Leben des Galilei* (three versions: 1943, 1947, 1954); shortly thereafter the somewhat slighter *Herr Puntila und sein Knecht Matti* (1948), and the very moving *Der kaukasische Kreidekreis* (1948).

As Brecht's theories of the drama are a most helpful though not infallible guide to his work, I shall briefly discuss them here. Central

---

* Dates given for Brecht's plays refer to their first performances. Several of the texts were subjected to extensive revision.

are the notions of the epic (i.e., narrative) theatre and the avoidance of empathy through *Verfremdung*. He rejected Aristotelian drama, as he called it, because of the catharsis it intends: when the spectator, 'identifying' with a character on the stage, is purged of emotion, he is rendered incapable, Brecht held, of either action or thought. Furthermore, rather than being spurred by a play, he enjoys it passively, wallowing in illusion and bourgeois luxury.

Accordingly, this dramatic illusion must be destroyed: an alert audience follows the story told to it, keen for its didactic implications. A whole battery of devices aims at 'distancing' the spectator. Characters step out of their roles, wear masks, or comment on the action; or a single narrator may be 'in charge' of a whole drama. Slogans are projected onto a screen or written on placards; some witty, some, in the more didactic works, almost insultingly simplistic, which again serves to 'alienate' the audience. The parody may be so obvious, as in the 'happy ending' of *Die Dreigroschenoper*, that the dullest public cannot miss its point. Similarly, a deliberate dissonance between a melodious tune and a sarcastic or sensationally shocking text keeps the spectators from reacting emotionally.

Precisely the best of Brecht's dramas, however, often conflict with these theories. The fortitude of Mother Courage, the goodness of the Chinese prostitute Shen Te, and above all the devotion of Grusche (in *Kreidekreis*) evoke our sympathy, quite in a traditional sense. We often agree with Brecht that outside pressures cause these heroines to act cruelly but maintain a 'sentimental' belief in their intrinsic goodness.

Mutter Courage, partly based on Grimmelshausen's novels of the Thirty Years War, shows Brecht's social criticism at its sharpest: war appears as a self-perpetuating institution.* In order to keep her canteen-wagon going, Mother Courage often finds it necessary to act ruthlessly. The spectator winces, but can hardly cast the first stone.

Der gute Mensch von Sezuan argues wittily that a good human being cannot survive in our world. If, however, he can split his personality and play a hard role in practical life, he can indulge himself in private kindliness. (This is also a basic theme of *Puntila*.)

---

* Her son Eilif is shot for performing, during an armistice, an act considered laudable in war—perhaps an echo of Unruh's *Ein Geschlecht*.

Accordingly, Shen Te survives by pretending on occasion to be her cousin Shui Ta, a ruthless exploiter. Again, we cannot feel alienated from a woman who has acted brutally only under compulsion; but we agree with Brecht that any world which subjects her to such compulsions must be changed.

Galilei derives its power from two sources mainly: the literally vital importance of its theme—the scientist's responsibility—and the rich, complex way in which the protagonist's character is developed. While Brecht may have been partly unaware of the autobiographical element in his portrait of Galileo, it is surely important. Quite apart from the traits of character possibly similar to Brecht's, the scientist's preference for an absolutist state over a capitalist democracy reflects the author's, as his Janus-faced attitude towards authority recalls Brecht's towards Ulbricht.

Galileo's empirically oriented genius and his great weakness stem from the same source, his sensuality.[3] To the end, he maintains his dual aspect. Although Brecht did write that Galileo 'becomes a criminal,'[4] the lapsed hero finished his greatest book during a time when he seemed a spineless slave of the Inquisition. The scorn of a former pupil changes back to admiration, but Galileo nevertheless feels that he is living in a moral gutter. His warning to his young friend, 'Take care when you pass through Germany,' poignantly recalls Brecht's exile. (*Galileo* was written in the United States.) Most poignant of all are the unmistakable references to the atomic bomb; Brecht implies that today's scientists, like Galileo, are betraying mankind.

In *Der kaukasische Kreidekreis*,[5] Brecht, made euphoric perhaps by the defeat of the Axis, writes with a warmth unique in his dramas. A Georgian folk singer sings the legend to illustrate, around 1945, a point of communist ethics to two groups of peasants. (The peasants have just decided a dispute according to this principle.) In a play within a play the legend or parable is acted out, with frequent comments and songs by the narrator.

This helps to distance the action of course, but one is certainly not *verfremdet vis-à-vis* the heroine Grusche, the most appealing person in Brecht. With quiet, modest heroism, she saves a baby abandoned during a revolution by its rich, incredibly vicious mother, and refuses to forsake it even when it seems that her loyalty, misunderstood, will drive her lover away. 'Schrecklich ist die Verführung zur Güte,' the singer warns her. In a parabolic trial scene, the judge[6] puts the baby in a chalk circle between Grusche and its mother; when the latter roughly pulls it to herself, the Solomonic judge awards the child to the gentle Grusche. At the end, the narrator sums up:

> Dass da gehören soll, was da ist, denen, die für es gut sind, also
> Die Kinder den Mütterlichen, damit sie gedeihen . . .
> Und das Tal den Bewässeren, damit es Frucht bringt.

Besides being framed by the contemporary action, the play is performed in a 'distanced' manner: the evil characters wear masks, there are many songs and ballads packed with ironic Brechtian insights, and perhaps the fact that the bad people are painted utterly black, over against Grusche's radiant whiteness, keeps the sophisticated spectator aware that it is all only a didactic fairy tale. Yet none of this 'distances' Grusche herself: she is as worthy of admiring sympathy as any heroine in German drama—and more credible than many of them.

Brecht's last years, spent mainly in East Berlin, were relatively unproductive and clouded by the position he took after the revolt of June, 1953. While he sympathized with the workers, he did not publish a satiric poem which he wrote against the Ulbricht government after that crisis. Like his Galileo, he played a double game, keeping property in the West and maintaining Austrian citizenship while profiting as a dramatist and director by the brilliant work of the Berlin Ensemble.

The leading dramatists to emerge after the Second World War are the Swiss writers Max Frisch (b. 1911) and Friedrich Dürrenmatt (b. 1921). Postwar German critics like to refer to Switzerland as an 'intact society' as—relatively at least—it indeed is; but the world which appears in the plays and other works of Frisch and Dürrenmatt is anything but solid, safe, or smug. The two men complement each other excellently: Frisch's central theme is the often tragic search of the individual for his true self, the struggle against the lie; Dürrenmatt, convinced that tragedy is impossible in an age lacking a coherent view of life and the world, focuses on the grotesque, the parodistic, and the absurd. Both, especially Dürrenmatt, are deeply indebted to Brecht in stage technique, content, and attitude.

The drama *Nun singen sie wieder* (1946), which he called an 'Attempt at a Requiem' for executed hostages, first established Frisch's European reputation. *Als der Krieg zu Ende war* also deals with the bitter aftermath of the war. To save her husband from punishment as a war criminal—he is one of those responsible for the slaughter of the Warsaw Jews—an admirable German woman has an affair with a colonel of the Russian army of occupation. Paradoxically, the fact that they communicate by gesture only, each ignorant of the other's language, makes for greater sincerity; genuine love springs from this relationship. Characteristically, Frisch has a moral point: in this case, 'Thou shalt make no graven image,'[7] that is, one must not damn a person for being German or Russian, or belonging to any other group. Actual crimes, however, like those of the German soldier here, must be condemned.

Frisch can also be light-hearted. In *Don Juan oder die Liebe zur Geometrie*, he parodies the myth of the great seducer: his Don Juan vastly prefers mathematics to women, but the aggressive females will not leave him in peace. The thesis of this play is that 'every man, when he is sober again, has a higher goal than woman'; but that life traps him and he marries. Finally Juan settles down with a former prostitute; at the end of the play, his wife is pregnant.

Biedermann und die Brandstifter (1958), like the war dramas, deals with a political but essentially moral theme. Biedermann is a prosperous, highly respected person—and infinitely inferior, in intelligence and human decency—to the adulteress in *Als der Krieg zu Ende war*. (His name recalls Hofmannsthal's Jedermann; but Frisch's 'worthy fellow' is much less attractive.) The prosperous Biedermann takes arsonists into his house as guests though they have told him precisely what they mean to do; they indeed live up to their word. One is reminded of the attitude of many 'respectable' Germans towards Hitler in 1933. Probably Frisch also had the threat of the atomic bomb in mind.

Frisch has also written novels; *Stiller* (1954) was his major success in this genre. The book is centred on the problem of identity: it is evidence of the new prestige of American literature in Europe that Frisch makes Irving's *Rip van Winkle* his 'objective correlative.' No doubt the hero's name is symbolic: it of course expresses his quiet passivity. As in the traditional Bildungsroman, Stiller's problem is

Nietzsche's: how do I 'become the person I am'? *Homo Faber* (1957), is the novel of a 'technical man,' utterly alienated from nature, incapable of love.

Like Frisch, Friedrich Dürrenmatt is extremely versatile, having produced, besides dramas, striking radio plays (*Hörspiele*), tales, critical essays, and even detective stories, as well as interesting drawings. In his comic techniques, Dürrenmatt shows a debt to Johann Nestroy, the nineteenth-century master of Austrian popular comedy. Mainly, however, he seems indebted, both in themes and theatrical devices, to more recent writers: Wedekind, Pirandello, Georg Kaiser, Thornton Wilder, and particularly to Brecht.

Dürrenmatt has written that in the modern world, the tragic hero is no longer viable. In the twentieth century, an Antigone would have been quietly disposed of by Creon's underlings.[8] Thus he writes comedies, but these plays are marked by a tragic sense[9] of decay and corruption. Finding the contemporary world absurd, he uses the techniques of *Verfremdung*, parody, and romantic irony. While his dramas often remind us of Brecht's, their tone is darker: Dürrenmatt has no faith in Marxist solutions, still less in the state as such. Yet he finds that courage and goodness are still possible, as evinced in the girl Kurubi in *Ein Engel kommt nach Babylon*, who seems to derive from Brecht's delightful Grusche. Often he returns to the 'antithesis of material prosperity and moral guilt,' as H. F. Garten has well put it.[10] Like Frisch, he is a master in unmasking the hypocrite.

Dürrenmatt's stage techniques are well suited to his belief that life is grotesque and absurd: he does not merely break the theatrical illusion; he shatters it to bits. Deliberate anachronisms and 'alienating' asides abound. His first play, *Es steht geschrieben* (1947) is wildly expressionistic; in *Die Ehe des Herrn Mississippi*, one window opens on a spring landscape, another on a wintry scene; the trees in *Der Besuch der alten Dame* (1956) are played by the burghers of Güllen. These are only a few examples of his virtuosity in tricks and 'gags'; at times his cleverness becomes wearying.

To give some account of Dürrenmatt's most striking dramas: his first clear success was *Romulus der Grosse* (1949; revised in the interest of greater seriousness in 1957), a rather Shavian treatment of the last Roman emperor of the West. In this 'unhistorical historical comedy,' as Dürrenmatt calls it, he changes the historical Romulus Augustulus, an ill-starred youth, into a wise, resigned man in his fifties, more interested in raising chickens than in glory. Among other alterations, he makes the German Odoacer, Romulus' successor, into a sophisticated and peace-loving person who becomes deeply devoted to the emperor. Anachronisms and 'wise-cracks' are frequent, but the play has a serious core: Romulus is vindicated. Rightly convinced that the empire is doomed, he avoids bloodshed by insisting on abdication.

Ein Engel kommt nach Babylon (1953; revised 1957) deals with the motivation for building the Tower of Babel. As Dürrenmatt's characteristic anachronisms make clear, Babylon is an image of contemporary society. Indeed, building the outrageous tower is clearly reminiscent of the manufacture of atomic bombs.[11] In Babylon, a totalitarian state, begging has been prohibited; God, however, sends to earth the beautiful maiden Kurubi to become the love of the last existing beggar. Even though King Nebukadnezar disguises himself as a mendicant, he is defeated by a genuine non-conformist, the beggar Akki. In his frustration, Nebukadnezar resolves to attack heaven by building the tower.

The most famous of Dürrenmatt's works, *Der Besuch der alten Dame*, is also his least bizarre and experimental drama. It is essentially a relentless, clear-cut study of extreme guilt and unflinching retribution. The billionaire heroine was betrayed as a young girl by Ill, now a respected burgher of Güllen, their native town; she senses moreover that Güllen 'society' as a whole shares the blame. Returned to this chronically depressed community, she offers the Gülleners an enormous reward for killing Ill, which they eventually do. Thus, by utterly corrupting them, she punishes the townspeople more severely than her former lover. Repeated flashes of wit illuminate this 'black' drama, which is marked as well by a pseudo-Sophoclean chorus and Dürrenmatt's usual 'gimmicks'—as well as by drastic, indeed sadistic touches. When the closing chorus invokes freedom and happiness, its cynical hypocrisy is almost unbearable:

> Bewahre die heiligen Güter uns, bewahre
> > Frieden
> Bewahre die Freiheit . . .
> Damit wir das Glückliche glücklich geniessen.

Dürrenmatt's radio play 'Die Panne' (1956) is admirably effective. While he employs some clever sound effects, the austerity of the form keeps his ingenuity within bounds. Alfredo Traps, a highly successful self-made man, finds refuge in a villa after his car has suffered a breakdown (_Panne_), only to find that he is trapped indeed. (The author seems to like bilingual puns: Ill in _Der Besuch_ . . . is truly sick.) Examined by a retired public prosecutor during a sumptuous banquet, Traps is led to confess that he has done away with his former chief by vicious though not illegal means. The retired judge condemns him to death, which Traps accepts with a sense of relief; but when morning comes, he finds that he is free: the condemnation was purely symbolic.* There is something Kleistian in Dürrenmatt's harsh contrast between the letter and the spirit, law and justice. Traps remains as ruthless as before; justice itself has broken down.

The first literary sensation of the postwar period was a new writer, Wolfgang Borchert (1921–47). An appealing figure, the youthful Borchert was twice imprisoned and once sentenced to death during the war for 'defeatist' remarks. When he went back to Hamburg—his native city, almost completely destroyed—he was already seriously ill. Yet the one play he lived to write—_Draussen vor der Tür_—made a deep impression. It presents, surrealistically, the plight of a soldier who returns to his ruined home from Siberian captivity and finds his wife with another man, his parents dead by suicide, his former colonel, an evil, brutal fellow, flourishing. Even his attempt to kill himself fails, and he finds that God is an old man who weeps at his inability to help. As the last touch suggests, the play is full of self-pity, as are the twelve stories collected as _Die Hundeblume_. Borchert, vastly overrated for a while, was indeed sentimental, but his work was the first wavering step towards recovery.

That recovery has since made remarkable progress. It is of course too early to attempt judgment on the writers who have become prominent only recently. Who would be rash enough to predict what works Günter Grass, say, or Martin Walser will yet produce, or how seriously the next generation will take the novels of Heinrich Böll or Gerd Gaiser? Yet it seems permissible to discuss briefly the authors who seem most promising at the present, even though,

* In the first—actually less pessimistic—version, Traps hangs himself.

because of lack of perspective, one's vision can be at best only partly correct. Some sins of omission and commission are inevitable.

To an amazing extent, the newest German literature is the product of the poets, dramatists, narrators, and critics associated in the famous *Gruppe 47*.[12] Shortly after the war a number of young writers and publicists met informally for mutual criticism of works read aloud, and above all for discussion of the state of German society, of present dangers and hopes for the future.

In fact, it was the banning of their journal, *Der Ruf*, in 1947, which had led to the founding of this loose association of idealistic young intellectuals; the name *Gruppe 47* came later. At the beginning, their aims were primarily political: they hoped to build an intellectual élite by democratic methods before attempting to re-educate the public. After their experiences during the Nazi period, they had no faith in mass organizations nor organizations as such. With this perhaps too 'élitist' approach, they soon came into conflict with the American military government. Paradoxically, the most influential force in modern German letters focused its energies on literature against the intention of its founders.

Soon the idea of directly influencing political life receeded, but the 'Group' has never countenanced any retreat into the world of aesthetic semblance: in contrast to the usual trend of German developments, its members do not make a virtue of being unpolitical. Even more remarkably, it never hardened into an organization. Although the critic and novelist Hans Werner Richter has been its guiding spirit since the beginning, it has no officers, dues,* nor memberships; its adherents vary from year to year: some drop out, new faces appear. Anti-authoritarian in orientation, it has by no means excluded writers from behind the 'Iron Curtain.' Often it has been described as a clique, but the list of the participants in its meetings reads like an honour roll of the talented new writers. It is by no means a complete one, however; it would be invidious to point out, in the brief account which follows, the relatively few names which do not appear there.

Of course the literary situation in 1947 was bleak indeed. Not merely were authors faced by ruins and poverty, and surrounded

---

* Since 1950 it has awarded annual literary prizes; the necessary funds are mainly contributed by publishers and radio stations.

by an atmosphere of defeat, shame, and resentment. The more sensitive perceived that the language itself had become corrupt: it was necessary to rebuild from the bottom, using the barest essentials. First of all, the last remnants of an evil—or even a merely sentimental—tradition must be cleared away: the term *Kahlschlag* furnished the appropriate metaphor. Günter Eich's poem 'Inventur' is a justly famous expression of the mood of the time. To quote two of its seven strophes:

> Dies ist meine Mütze
> dies ist mein Mantel,
> hier mein Rasierzeug
> im Beutel aus Leinen

> .   .   .   .

> Die Bleistiftmine
> lieb ich am meisten:
> tags schreibt sie mir Verse,
> die nachts ich erdacht.

> .   .   .   .

The speaker no longer has even his mechanical pencil, only a package of leads; but there is no hint of self-pity.

In twenty-four meetings from 1947 through 1962, there were some 400 readings; they still continue. Each author must face severe criticism, for the 'Group' regards harshness as the badge of integrity. In its earlier years, a writer had to break off if the audience made the 'thumbs-down' gesture; and the seat the reader takes is still called the electric chair. Unlike the *Sturm und Drang*, the naturalists, and other German literary movements, *Gruppe 47* takes no line:[13] it has welcomed writers as antipodal as Günter Grass and Paul Celan, Heinrich Böll and Uwe Johnson. It includes both a number of realistic prose writers and experimentalists in both prose and verse. Whatever the importance of this or that member, the very existence of the 'Group' as an institution is a heartening fact.

While the postwar drama has been dominated by Brecht, Frisch, and Dürrenmatt, two works of the early Sixties deserve mention: Martin Walser's *Eiche und Angora* (1962) and Rolf Hochhuth's internationally famous *Der Stellvertreter* (1963). The former deals with the effects of the war and the concentration camps; the latter, primarily with the camps themselves—and with the bitterly debated question of Pope Pius XII's attitude towards the fate of the European Jews. Both, then, have themes of almost unbearable painfulness. Walser tries to achieve 'distance' by abundant use of irony and wit; Hochhuth uses a frankly old-fashioned, Schillerian approach: the plots and counterplots are as gripping as those of *Kabale und Liebe* or *Don Carlos*. He has been reproached for 'painting in black and white,' but the stark opposition of light and dark is inherent in the subject itself.

A characteristic phenomenon of recent years is the *Hörspiel*, or radio play. Notoriously, writing for the wireless tends to be a subliterary exercise, but obviously need not be one: besides Frisch and Dürrenmatt, a number of respected figures, including Ilse Aichinger, Böll, Eich, Siegfried Lenz, and Wolfgang Weyrauch, have contributed to the new genre. A genuine *Hörspiel* compares to 'legitimate' drama much as a novella to a novel.

Perhaps the most striking achievements have been made in the novel. Here the books of Grass, Johnson, the very fertile Böll, Walser, and Gerd Gaiser have been outstanding, along with those of various older writers.

Although hardly a great artist, Heinrich Böll, (b. 1917) is clearly a gifted one. A convincing realist, he seems to have learned more from Hemingway than from Borchert. (The latter is his predecessor in what some critics have sarcastically labelled *Trümmerliteratur*.) A committed moralist, radically Christian, Böll has presented both the drabness of the immediate postwar period and the materialism of the 'economic miracle' in *Und sagte kein einziges Wort* (1953) and later novels. *Wo warst du, Adam?* (1951) has as its theme that alibis—in this case, service as a soldier—are no excuse.

Uwe Johnson (b. 1934) uses an experimental style to evoke a Kafkaesque world in which nothing is sure. A voluntary exile from the 'German Democratic Republic,' he shows the dream- or nightmare-like quality of life under a totalitarian régime; but existence in the West appears, in his rendering, almost equally baffling. The title of his *Mutmassungen über Jakob* (1959) is especially to the point: one can make only conjectures. Similarly, in *Das dritte Buch über Achim*, published two years later, the book referred to in the title cannot be written: it would be impossible to publish the objective truth about Achim, a famous East German athlete, even if it could be ascertained.

A lavishly gifted writer, Günter Grass (b. 1927) owes much to Grimmelshausen, Jean Paul, and apparently to Joyce. His prose is rich in fantastic devices, plays on words, and comic or grotesque effects. In *Die Blechtrommel* (1959), the brilliant, scurrilous dwarf Oskar Matzerath encounters and reacts against the world of Nazism, war, and the ensuing period. His potent, often destructive drum seems to be a symbol of Grass's own satiric art. *Hundejahre* (1963) is an equally varied and virtuoso novel but lacks the sharp focus of its predecessor.

The novella, tale, and 'short story'—the last a postwar importation—are cultivated by many writers, most notably perhaps by Böll. Grass's symbolic *Katz und Maus* is his most disciplined narrative.

Like the prose narrative, the lyric has undergone a remarkable revival since the war. One is reminded of the poetic renascence of the Nineties, though it is impossible to know whether this renewed flowering will be equally splendid. Again, the stimulus has come largely from other literatures—from the French symbolists and sur-realists primarily, but also from Eliot, Auden, and Lorca. Culturally isolated for twelve years, German poets have been particularly open to international influences. There seem to be two main streams: one tends towards 'pure poetry,' a more or less autonomous arrange-ment of images or 'ciphers,' often very difficult to grasp; the other earthier, more direct, often satiric, bent on establishing a thesis. The former derives mainly from the twentieth-century French lyric and from Benn's attempt to practise 'absolute' poetry; the latter, starting with the *Kahlschlag* poetry of the mid- and late Forties, owes much to Brecht. Paul Celan and Karl Krolow are outstanding among the 'absolute' writers; Eich, Grass, and Hans Magnus Enzensberger among the more down-to-earth. Of course, the distinction is not absolute: Celan's most powerful poem, 'Todesfuge,' is a direct evo-cation of the concentration camps; and some of the more satiric groups have written in 'ciphers' as well; thus Grass writes 'absurd' poems, some of them amusingly nonsensical. In a longer book one would consider the work of all these poets, and also that of Ingeborg Bachmann, Marie Luise Kaschnitz, Peter Huchel, Johannes Bobrowski, and possibly a few others. Here the discussion must be limited to the two most gifted: Celan and Ingeborg Bachmann, who combines elements of both major strains in her poetry.[14]

Paul Celan was born in 1920, in Rumania, of German-speaking parents who were murdered in a Nazi concentration camp. Thus the line in 'Todesfuge'—

Der Tod ist ein Meister aus Deutschland—

expresses most intense personal experience. Now a French citizen, Celan lives in Paris.

Celan has published four major volumes of verse: *Mohn und Gedächtnis* (1952), *Von Schwelle zu Schwelle* (1955), *Sprachgitter* (1959) and *Die Niemandsrose* (1962). In addition he has made free translations of poems by Rimbaud, Valéry, Blok, Mandelshtam, and others. He owes much to the French symbolists, to expressionistic writers, especially Trakl, to the surrealists, and to Rilke; also to the Hasidic tradition and to Martin Buber (the search for a dialogue is important in his work).

In line with the symbolistic tradition many of his poems deal with poetry itself. He is obsessed with the difficulty of expression and communication: when words decay, language itself becomes a barrier to communication, as the title *Sprachgitter* implies. His other major themes are love, memory and forgetfulness, and death—in particular, the death of his mother.

As J. M. Lyon has shown,[15] Celan presents in his poems an 'internal landscape'—the term recalls Rilke's *Weltinnenraum*—in which natural objects and animals function as images or ciphers. A difficult poet, Celan arranges his poems associatively; he makes frequent use of paradoxical phrases like 'Zwischen immer and nie' and of deliberate ambiguities. He likes to link together images from different realms, as in the line

sieben Rosen später rauscht der Brunnen.

Although he is not a revolutionary in language, he likes to coin such compounds as *Schattenfisch*.

Some commentators hold that Celan's poems are unduly abstract. While most of them do demand repeated close readings, they are not enigmas to be puzzled out, but genuinely lyrical. To quote one brief poem:

> Sie kämmt ihr Haar wie mans den Toten kämmt:
> sie trägt den blauen Scherben unterm Hemd.
>
> Sie trägt den Scherben Welt an einer Schnur.
> Sie weiss die Worte, doch sie lächelt nur.
>
> Sie mischt ihr Lächeln in den Becher Wein:
> du musst ihn trinken, in der Welt zu sein.
>
> Du bist das Bild, das ihr der Scherben zeigt,
> wenn sie sich sinnend übers Leben neigt.

Here, as in many of Picasso's paintings, the distortion of reality produces beauty.* It is unlikely that Celan will be widely read, but still more unlikely that his work will be forgotten.

The poetry of the Austrian writer Ingeborg Bachmann is a unique combination of experimental and traditional elements. By no means old-fashioned, it makes use of familiar images and *topoi*, and is thus more easily grasped than the verse of many of her contemporaries. Like Celan, Frau Bachmann uses both free verse and the more conventional forms. While she owes much to Rilke and Hölderlin, she is highly original.

Frau Bachmann has written stories and radio plays, but her reputation is based essentially on two brief volumes of lyrics, *Die gestundete Zeit* (1953) and *Anrufung des grossen Bären* (1956). Her major themes are the emptiness of the universe, of life itself and man's consequent sense of *Angst*. (She wrote a doctoral dissertation on Heidegger.) Only in 'the word,' in poetry, can man find refuge: he discovers an authentic, ordered existence only 'in der schönen Sprache/im reinen Sein.' In the earlier volume, a tone of lamentation prevails. A number of these poems are comments on the age—*Zeitgedichte*—like the very dark poem 'Grosse Landschaft bei Wien.' She writes repeatedly of the impossibility or near-impossibility of love—

* Celan has translated Picasso's strange little play *Le désir attrapé par la queue*.

> Die Liebe graste nicht mehr
> die Glocken waren verhallt
> und die Büschel verhärmt.

Anrufung des grossen Bären is marked by a tone of praise, but the sense of dread nevertheless remains: the first line of the title poem reads:

> Grosser Bär, komm herab, zottige Nacht.

Frau Bachmann's very bold imagery typically combines, in many of her poems, negative and positive symbols. Appropriately, her extremely dialectic mind makes use of compound images, like *verschlammte Sterne* or 'Lösch die Lupinen.'[16] The prevailing tone is one of sadness—

> Nebelland hab ich gesehen
> Nebelherz hab ich gegessen—

but not of despondency.

Literary criticism has also experienced a revival, though a rather modest one. Here, because of Goebbels' dictatorship over the journals, the Germans had lagged particularly far behind: most critics were reduced to propagandists. Belatedly German intellectuals learned of the 'new criticism' and rediscovered close reading: for a long while, interpretation of texts seemed to be the one, magical method. Now a more sophisticated attitude prevails, though no Lessing, Schlegel, or Kraus has appeared on the scene. Among the leading critics are Hans Werner Richter, Hans Egon Holthusen, Walter Jens, Walter Höllerer, Paul Rilla, and Hans Mayer—the last, though a confirmed Marxist, an emigrant from East Germany.

Surely it would have been rash to predict, in 1945, the recovery which has actually taken place. The development is more surprising, if less spectacular, than the 'economic miracle.' Although no writer of dominating genius has emerged, there are a number of highly gifted authors. A limiting factor is the near-destruction of writers as a functioning, more or less integrated group and of the broad, cultivated literary public by terror, emigration, and war. At best, it will take decades to restore the situation completely; the cafés of Vienna, Berlin, and Munich are no longer teeming with poets, artists, musicians, and their admirers. Yet literature in German has again a distinct and respected voice in the international chorus.

Notes

1. Claude David, in *Von Richard Wagner zu Bertolt Brecht* (Frankfurt a. M. and Hamburg, 1964; originally published as part of *Histoire de la littérature allemande* [Paris, 1959], p. 97), points out that no first-rate German author was born between 1845 and 1862.

2. Hermann Hesse wrote some very pleasant lyrics, but he was awarded a Nobel Prize primarily for his fiction.

3. See Heinrich Henel's distinguished work, *The Poetry of Conrad Ferdinand Meyer* (Madison, Wis., 1954).

4. David, pp. 72–74.

5. Two recent works of great distinction suggest that this may indeed be the case: Harry Levin's *The Gates of Horn* (New York, 1963) and Ernest J. Simmons' *Introduction to Russian Realism* (Bloomington, 1965).

6. See Peter Demetz, *Formen des Realismus: Theodor Fontane* (Munich, 1964).

7. *The Tribune Almanac for 1860* (New York), p. 46, notes that in 1850 the German population was less than that of France.

8. R. H. Fife, *The German Empire between Two Wars* (New York, 1916), pp. 160f.

9. See Walter Linden, *Naturalismus* (Leipzig, 1936), pp. 7f. (*Deutsche Literatur*, Reihe 'Vom Naturalismus zur neuen Volksdichtung.')

10. The term suggests comparison with the liberal 'Young German' school of the 1830's and 1840's.

11. Taine's triad derives from Herder; see Henri Tronchon, *La fortune intellectuelle de Herder en France* (Paris, 1920).

12. See W. H. Root, 'German Naturalism' in *Columbia Dictionary of Modern European Literature* (New York, 1947), p. 319.

13. See Root's article 'Optimism in the Naturalistic Weltanschauung,' *Germanic Review*, XIV (1939), 54–63.

14. The once famous pseudo-naturalistic dramas of Hermann Sudermann are no longer taken seriously.

15. Compare Wolfgang Kayser's remarks in his *Die Vortragsreise* (Bern, 1958), pp. 222, 226.

16. Marianne Ordon, 'Unconscious Contents in "Bahnwärter Thiel",' *Germanic Review*, XXVI (1951), 223–29.

17. (The theory of the *Mittelachse*.)

18. Margaret Sinden also suggests that it owes a debt to Tolstoy in her *Gerhart Hauptmann: The Prose Plays* (Toronto, 1957), p. 18.

19. Sinden, p. 37.

20. Sinden, pp. 69, 75.

21. See Karl S. Guthke, *Gerhart Hauptmann* (Göttingen, 1961), pp. 72–78.

22. See Hermann J. Weigand in PMLA, LVII (1942), 1160–95; LVIII (1943), 797–848.

CHAPTER 2

1. See Bahr's *Die Überwindung des Naturalismus*.

2. Contrast Crane Brinton's *Nietzsche* (Cambridge, Mass., 1941) to Walter Kaufmann's *Nietzsche* (Princeton, 1950).

3. Actually, Friedrich Schlegel and others discovered the 'Dionysiac' element long before Nietzsche.

4. See Gisela Deesz, *Die Entwicklung des Nietzsche-Bildes in Deutschland* (Würzburg, 1933) and Ingeborg Beithan, *Nietzsche als Umwerter der deutschen Literatur* (Heidelberg, 1933).

5. See Helmut Rehder in *Monatshefte*, XXXVI (1944), 438, citing Nietzsche (Kröner ed., 1919), XVI, 386.

6. 'Eternal return' is not an original concept of Nietzsche's, despite his claims to the contrary.

7. Victor A. Oswald, jr., 'The Old Age of Young Vienna,' *Germanic Review*, XXVII (1952), 192.

8. See *Die neue Rundschau*, LXVI (1955), 97.

9. See Wolfgang Kayser, *Die Vortragsreise* (Bern, 1958), p. 300.

10. Cf. Walter Jens, *Hofmannsthal und die Griechen* (Tübingen, 1955), p. 73.

11. Jens, p. 66.

12. *Insel-Almanach* (1929), pp. 106f.

13. Soergel-Hohoff, *Dichtung und Dichter der Zeit*, (2nd ed. Düsseldorf, 1961–63), I, 471f.

14. Richard Alewyn, 'Hofmannsthals Wandlung,' in his *Über Hugo von Hofmannsthal* (Göttingen, 1958), pp. 142–60.

CHAPTER 3

1. David, p. 117f.

2. 'Und von neuem ein Jahr unserer Seele beginnt'—the last line of the elegy 'Menons Klagen um Diotima.'

3. Soergel-Hohoff, I, 407.

4. See W. F. Michael in *Modern Language Forum*, XXXV (1950), 35–38.

5. See Alfred Bäumler, *Männerbund und Wissenschaft* (Berlin, 1937).

6. Significantly a poem included in George's *Das neue Reich* mentions the First War in a way implying that a second one would be a Good Thing.

7. Bernhard Blume, 'Ding und Ich in Rilke's *Neuen Gedichten*,' *Modern Language Notes*, LXVII (1952), 217–24.

8. Soergel-Hohoff, I, 285.

9. See Harry Slochower, *Richard Dehmel* (Dresden, 1928), p. 116f.

10. H. G. Wendt, *Max Dauthendey, Poet-Philosopher* (New York, 1936), p. 62.

11. See Leo Spitzer in Sperber and Spitzer, *Motiv und Wort* (Leipzig, 1918), pp. 53–123.

CHAPTER 4

1. See Ulrich Weisstein, *Heinrich Mann* (Tübingen, 1962), p. 105.

2. The historical Savonarola appears in Mann's closet drama *Fiorenza* (1905).

3. Thus Vernon Venable, 'Poetic Reason in Thomas Mann,' *Virginia Quarterly Review*, XIV (1938), 61–76; André von Gronicka, 'Myth and Psychology,' *Germanic Review*, XXXI (1956), 191–205.

4. Theodore Ziolkowski, *Hermann Hesse* (Princeton, 1965), p. 4.

5. Ziolkowski, p. 25.

6. See Eliot's note on *The Waste Land*, ll. 366–76.

CHAPTER 5

1. The term was first used in German, apparently, by Wilhelm Worringer, in the periodical *Der Sturm* (1911), to describe French paintings. See Fritz Martini in *Deutsche Literatur im zwanzigsten Jahrhundert* (Heidelberg, 1954), p. 107.

2. Musil, *Der Mann ohne Eigenschaften* (Hamburg, 1952), p. 56.

3. Cf. Wolfgang Paulsen, *Aktivismus und Expressionismus* (Berlin and Leipzig, 1935).

4. Edschmid, *Über den Expressionismus in der Literatur* (Berlin, 1919), p. 52.

5. Pinthus, *Menschheitsdämmerung* (Berlin, 1919), pp. xivf.

6. *Minna von Barnhelm*, II, 1; cf. Walter H. Sokel, *The Writer in Extremis* (Stanford, 1959), pp. 67–75.

7. Richard Samuel and R. H. Thomas, *Expressionism in German Life, Literature, and the Theatre* (Cambridge, 1939), p. 9.

8. Soergel-Hohoff, I, 668.

9. See H. F. Garten, *Modern German Drama* (New York, 1962), p. 89.

10. Sokel, p. 62.

11. Sokel, p. 66.

12. See Heidegger, 'Georg Trakl,' *Merkur*, VII (1953), 253.

13. See Huelsenbeck (ed.), *Dada* (Hamburg, 1964), p. 30.

14. Quoted in Soergel-Hohoff, II, 311.

15. *Ibid.*, p. 318.

16. Similarly, expressionistic painting and sculpture have 'worn' better than most expressionistic literature.

17. See the final scene of Goethe's *Egmont* (1787).

18. See Brian Kenworthy, *Georg Kaiser* (Oxford, 1957), p. 30.

19. Garten, p. 135.

CHAPTER 6

1. Only Amalia presumes to judge, and she is then ostracized.

2. See Anders' *Franz Kafka*, trans. by A. Steer and A. K. Thorlby (London, 1960).

3. For an excellent, thorough discussion of this story, see Heinz Politzer, *Franz Kafka, Parable and Paradox* (Ithaca, N. Y., 1962), pp. 98–115.

4. Politzer, p. 124.

5. It has been argued that the chapters of both *Der Prozess* and *Amerika* were wrongly arranged by Brod. See Herman Uyttersprot, *Eine neue Ordnung der Werke Kafkas?* (Antwerp, 1957).

6. Kierkegaardian interpreters claim that, since ethics and theology are completely separate, the immorality of the Court does not diminish its religious value; but this is unconvincing. Although Kafka read some of Kierkegaard, he was not persuaded.

7. 'Before the Law' (which seems to derive from Strindberg's *A Dream Play*) has Kafka's *imprimatur*: it was published in *Ein Landarzt*, a collection of his stories.

8. See Ingeborg Henel in *Deutsche Vierteljahresschrift*, XXXVII (1963), 50–70.

9. Either, as Politzer argues (p. 184), this shows that the Court is condemned by its own standards, or Kafka wished to leave his readers perpetually puzzled, or both.

10. See Norbert Fürst, *Die offenen Geheimtüren Franz Kafkas* (Heidelberg, 1956), p. 38.

11. Politzer, pp. 229–234

12. *Ibid.*, p. 258.

13. Heller, *The Disinherited Mind*, p. 175.

14. See Howard Nemerov, 'The Quester Hero' (Bowdoin prize essay, Harvard, 1940).

15. The puns and plays on words in the seventh chapter recall Joyce, but Mann denied having read *Ulysses* by that time. Undoubtedly he knew Schnitzler's 'Leutnant Gustl.'

16. Ziolkowski, p. 232.

17. See W. K. Pfeiler, *War and the German Mind* (New York, 1941).

18. See Burton Pike, *Robert Musil* (Ithaca, N.Y., 1961), p. 197

19. Soergel-Hohoff, II, 518.

20. Theodore Ziolkowski, *Hermann Broch* (New York and London, 1964), p. 42.

CHAPTER 7

1. Rather curiously, Hauptmann's plays in dialect generally have the firmest linguistic texture.

2. See Hilde Cohn in *Monatshefte*, XLIV (1952), 257–69.

3. See Paul Requadt, 'Hugo von Hofmannsthal,' in *Deutsche Literatur des zwanzigsten Jahrhunderts*, p. 60.

4. Cf. especially *Der Tor und der Tod* and *Der Schwierige*.

5. See Edgar Hederer, *Hugo von Hofmannsthal* (Frankfurt a. M., 1960), p. 69.

6. David, p. 134.

7. See Romano Guardini, *Rilkes Deutung des Daseins* (München, 1953), p. 30.

8. Werner Günther, *Weltinnenraum* (Bern-Leipzig, 1943), pp. 136f.

9. See Liselotte Dieckmann in *Modern Language Quarterly*, XII (1951), 322f.

10. Walter Muschg, *Von Trakl zu Brecht, Dichter des Expressionismus* (München, 1961), p. 180.

11. See Leopold Liegler's analysis of Kraus's language in *Karl Kraus und sein Werk* (Wien, 1933), pp. 285–386.

12. Liegler, p. 77.

INTERCHAPTER

1. See H. R. Klieneberger in *Monatshefte*, LVII (1965), 171–80, esp. 174 ff.

2. See Charles W. Hoffmann's excellent monograph *Opposition Poetry in Nazi Germany* (Berkeley and Los Angeles, 1962), p. 40.

3. Hoffmann, pp. 103–61.

4. See Viereck's *Metapolitics* (New York, 1941).

CHAPTER 8

1. *Primal Vision*, pp. xxif.

2. See Bernhard Blume in *Euphorion*, XLVII (1954), 71–89.

3. See Hans Eichner, *Four German Writers* (Toronto, 1964), p. 70.

4. Quoted in Martin Esslin, *Brecht: The Man and his Work* (New York, 1960), p. 258.

5. Brecht used a Chinese story which the expressionist Klabund (Alfred Henschke) had treated in his drama *Der chinesische Kreidekreis* (1925).

6. Esslin (p. 257) suggests that this judge is another self-portrait: he is shrewd, is often immoral, and his sympathies are with the poor.

7. Hans Bänzinger, *Frisch und Dürrenmatt*, (2nd ed., Bern und München [1962]) p. 62.

8. Dürrenmatt, *Theaterprobleme* (Zurich, 1955), pp. 43f.

9. See Adolf Klarmann in *Tulane Review*, IV (1960), 77–104.

10. In the introduction to his edition of *Romulus der Grosse* (Boston, Mass., 1962), p. ix.

11. Klarmann, p. 96.

12. See the authoritative *Almanach der Gruppe 47; 1947–1962*, ed. Hans Werner Richter and Walter Mannzen. Neuwied, 1962.

13. See Hans Mayer in *Almanach der Gruppe*, pp. 37–39.

14. See S. S. Prawer in *German Life and Letters*, XIII (1959–60), 18–26.

15. In '"Nature" in the Imagery of Bachmann, Celan, and Krolow,' Diss. Harvard, 1962, pp. 115–20, 213f.

16. See Lyon, pp. 75f.

Bibliography

A. HISTORIES OF GERMAN LITERATURE, ETC.

Bithell, Jethro. *Modern German Literature*, third edition. London: Methuen, 1959.

David, Claude. *L'Époque Bismarckienne et l'Allemagne Contemporaine.* Paris: Éditions Montaigne, 1959. (= vol. V of *Histoire de la Littérature Allemande*, ed. Fernand Mossé.) German translation: *Von Richard Wagner zu Bertolt Brecht.* Frankfurt a. M.: Fischer Bücherei, 1964.

Handbuch der deutschen Gegenwartsliteratur, ed. Herman Kunisch. München: Nymphenburger Verlagshandlung, 1965.

Kleines literarisches Lexikon, second edition, ed. Wolfgang Kayser. Bern: Francke, 1953.

Lange, Victor. *Modern German Literature 1870–1940*. Ithaca, N.Y.: Cornell Univ. Press, 1945.

Robertson, J. G. *A History of German Literature*, fourth edition, rev. by Edna Purdie. Edinburgh: W. Blackwood, 1962.

Soergel, Albert and Curt Hohoff. *Dichtung und Dichter der Zeit*. 2 vols. Düsseldorf: Bagel, 1961, 1963.

B. Works concerning Literary Periods

1. *Naturalism:*

Naturalismus, ed. Walter Linden (in the series *Deutsche Literatur*). Leipzig: Reclam, 1936.

Röhl, Hans. *Der Naturalismus*. Leipzig: Quelle & Meyer, 1927.

Root, W. H. 'German Naturalism and its Literary Predecessors,' in *Germanic Review*, XXIII (1948), 115–24.

2. *Neo-Romanticism and Impressionism:*

Bowra, C. M. *The Heritage of Symbolism*. London: Macmillan, 1943.

Eindrucks- und Symbolkunst, ed. Walter Linden (*Deutsche Literatur*). Leipzig: Reclam, 1940.

Hamann, Richard & J. Hermand. *Der Impressionismus*. Berlin: Akademie Verlag, 1960.

3. *Expressionism:*

Diebold, Bernhard. *Anarchie im Drama*, fourth edition. Berlin-Wilmersdorf: H. Keller, 1928.

Menschheitsdämmerung, ed. Kurt Pinthus. Hamburg: Rowohlt, 1960 [originally 1919].

Samuel, Richard and R. H. Thomas. *Expressionism in German Life, Literature, and the Theatre*. Cambridge, [Eng.]: Heffer & Sons, 1939.

Sokel, Walter. *The Writer in Extremis: Expressionism in Twentieth-century German Literature*. Stanford, Calif.: Stanford Univ. Press, 1959.

4. *From 1933 to 1945:*

Hoffmann, Charles W. *Opposition Poetry in Nazi Germany*. Berkeley: Univ. of California Press, 1962.

Sternfeld, Wilhelm & Eva Tiedemann. *Deutsche Exilliteratur, 1933–45*. Heidelberg: Schneider, 1962.

Strothmann, Dietrich. *Nationalsozialistische Literaturpolitik*, second edition. Bonn: Bouvier, 1963.

5. *The Post-Nazi Generation:*

Almanach der Gruppe 47, 1947–62, ed. H. W. Richter. and W. Mannzen Neuwied: Luchterhand, 1962.

C. Books about Specific Authors

Benn:

Benn, Gottfried. *Primal Vision*, ed. Hans Ashton, Norfolk, Conn.: New Directions, n.d.

C. Books about Specific Authors (continued)

Brecht:

Esslin, Martin. *Brecht: the Man and His Work*. New York, Doubleday, 1960.

Willett, John. *The Theatre of Bertolt Brecht*. Norfolk, Conn.: New Directions, 1959.

Broch:

Ziolkowski, Theodore. *Hermann Broch*. New York and London: Columbia Univ. Press, 1964.

Dürrenmatt: (and Frisch)

Bänzinger, Hans. *Dürrenmatt und Frisch*, second edition. Bern: Francke, 1962.

Frisch: see under Dürrenmatt.

George:

David, Claude. *Stefan George: Son œuvre poétique*. Lyon: IAC, 1952.

Goldsmith, Ulrich. *Stefan George: A Study of his Early Work*. Boulder: Colorado Univ. Press, 1959.

Hauptmann:

Guthke, Karl S. *Gerhart Hauptmann*. Göttingen: Vandenhoeck & Ruprecht, 1961.

Sinden, Margaret. *Gerhart Hauptmann: The Prose Plays*. Toronto: Toronto Univ. Press, 1957.

Hesse:

Ball, Hugo. *Hermann Hesse: Sein Leben und sein Werk*, second edition. (Continued by Anni Carlsson and Otto Basler.) Zürich: Fretz & Wasmuth, 1947.

Ziolkowski, Theodore. *The Novels of Hermann Hesse*. Princeton: Princeton Univ. Press, 1965.

Hofmannsthal:

Alewyn, Richard. *Über Hugo von Hofmannsthal*, second edition. Göttingen: Vandenhoeck & Ruprecht, 1960.

Kafka:

Emrich, Wilhelm. *Franz Kafka*. Bonn: Athenäum, 1958.

Politzer, Heinz. *Franz Kafka: Parable and Paradox*. Ithaca, N.Y.: Cornell Univ. Press, 1962.

Sokel, Walter. *Franz Kafka: Tragik und Ironie*. München: Langen-Müller, 1964.

Wagenbach, Klaus. *Franz Kafka: Eine Biographie seiner Jugend*. Bern: Francke, 1958.

Kraus:

Liegler, Leopold. *Karl Kraus und sein Werk*. Wien: R. Lányi, 1920; 2nd ed., 1933.

C. BOOKS ABOUT SPECIFIC AUTHORS (continued)

Mann, Heinrich:

Weisstein, Ulrich. *Heinrich Mann*. Tübingen: Niemeyer, 1962.

Mann, Thomas:

Bürgin, Hans and Hans-Otto Mayer. *Thomas Mann: Eine Chronik seines Lebens*. Frankfurt a. M.: S. Fischer, 1965.

Hatfield, Henry. *Thomas Mann*, second edition. Norfolk, Conn.: New Directions, 1962.

Heller, Erich. *The Ironic German: A Study of Thomas Mann*. Frome and London: Butler and Tanner, 1958.

Thomas, R. H. *Thomas Mann*. Oxford: Clarendon Press, 1956.

Musil:

Kaiser, Ernst & Eithne Wilkins. *Robert Musil: Eine Einführung in das Werk*. Stuttgart: Kohlhammer, 1962.

Pike, Burton. *Robert Musil: An Introduction to His Work*. Ithaca, N.Y.: Cornell Univ. Press, 1961.

Nietzsche:

Brinton, Crane. *Nietzsche*. Cambridge, Mass.: Harvard Univ. Press, 1941.

Kaufmann, Walter. *Nietzsche: Philosopher, Psychologist, Antichrist*. Princeton: Princeton Univ. Press, 1950.

Rilke:

Butler, E. M. *Rainer Maria Rilke*. Cambridge, [Eng.]: At the University Press, 1941.

Guardini, Romano. *Rainer Maria Rilkes Deutung des Daseins*. München: Kösel, 1953.

Peters, H. F. *Rainer Maria Rilke: Masks and the Man*. Seattle: Univ. of Washington Press, 1960.

Wood, Frank. *Rainer Maria Rilke: The Ring of Forms*. Minneapolis: Univ. of Minnesota Press, 1958.

Schnitzler:

Blume, Bernhard. *Das Weltbild Arthur Schnitzlers*. Stuttgart: Knöller, 1936.

Trakl:

Killy, Walther. *Über Georg Trakl*, second edition. Göttingen: Vandenhoeck & Ruprecht, 1962.

Wedekind:

Kutscher, Artur. *Frank Wedekind: Sein Leben und seine Werke*. 3 vols. München: G. Müller, 1922–31.

Index

This index does not include every minor reference to all persons mentioned. The more important treatments of a given writer are indicated by bold-face type. As noted in the preface, the dates of all works discussed in the book are given here.